Peripheral Vision

Platform Studies
Nick Montfort and Ian Bogost, editors

Peripheral Vision

Bell Labs, the S-C 4020, and the Origins of Computer Art

Zabet Patterson

The MIT Press   Cambridge, Massachusetts   London, England

This book was set in Filosofia and Helvetica Neue by Toppan Best-set Premedia Limited.

Library of Congress Cataloging-in-Publication Data

Patterson, Zabet.
Peripheral vision : Bell Labs, the S-C 4020 and the origins of computer art / Zabet Patterson.
    pages   cm. — (Platform studies)
Includes bibliographical references and index.
ISBN 978-0-262-02952-0 (hardcover : alk. paper)
ISBN 978-0-262-54882-3 (paperback)
1. Computer art. 2. Computer peripherals. 3. AT & T Bell Laboratories. I. Title.
N7433.8.P378   2015
776—dc23
2015002000

For A

Contents

Series Foreword

How can someone create a breakthrough game for a mobile phone or a compelling work of art for an immersive three-dimensional environment without understanding that the mobile phone and the 3D environment are different sorts of computing platforms? The best game artists, writers, programmers, and designers are well aware of how certain platforms facilitate certain types of computational expression and innovation. Likewise, computer science and engineering have long considered how underlying computing systems can be analyzed and improved. As important as scientific and engineering approaches are and as significant as work by creative artists has been, there is also much to be learned from the sustained, intensive, humanistic study of digital media. We believe it is time for humanists to consider the lowest level of computing systems to understand their relationship to culture and creativity.

The Platform Studies book series has been established to promote the investigation of underlying computing systems and the ways that they enable, constrain, shape, and support the creative work that is done on them. The series investigates the foundations of digital media—the computing systems, both hardware and software, that developers and users depend on for artistic, literary, and gaming development. Books in the series will vary in their approaches but will share certain features:

- A focus on a single platform or a closely related family of platforms,
- Technical rigor and in-depth investigation of how computing technologies work, and

- An awareness of and discussion of how computing platforms exist in a context of culture and society, being developed based on cultural concepts and then contributing to culture in a variety of ways—for instance, by affecting how people perceive computing.

Acknowledgments

This project first took form at the University of California, Berkeley, in the marvelous interdisciplinary environment that extended there across the departments of Rhetoric and Film Studies, Art History, and Performance Studies. I owe an incredible debt to Kaja Silverman and Shannon Jackson; I can only offer my heartfelt thanks. I am also profoundly grateful to Linda Williams and Greg Niemeyer for their efforts on my behalf. While at Berkeley, I participated in an extraordinary community that shaped my thinking: Patrick Anderson, Scott Combs, Jessica Davies, Meredith Hoy, Homay King, Eve Meltzer, Andrew Moisey, John Muse, Ara Osterweil, Kris Paulson, Domietta Torlasco, and Heather Warren-Crow, among many others, deserve special acknowledgement. At Stony Brook, I have been fortunate to find a home with wonderful colleagues in Art and cDACT.

This book would not have happened without Ian Bogost, who saw the possibilities in this project, and, with Nick Montfort, stewarded it through the initial stages at MIT Press. I am grateful to Doug Sery, and the team of editors at the MIT Press, as well as to the anonymous editors solicited by the MIT Press, whose insightful comments clarified my thinking, and made this a much better piece of work.

My parents have offered years and hours of endless patience and support. Matthew, laughter and learning a little something, always. My extended family has offered love and understanding. But the days, weeks, and minutes have belonged to my smaller family: Perdita, Surya, Maya, and, above all, Andrew.

Introduction

In the late 1950s and 1960s, mainframes dominated computing. Their name came from the large metal frames in which banks of circuits were mounted. They were more architecture than object, and their cost was commensurate. As such, these computers were the exclusive province of governmental military agencies, university research centers, and a few of the largest corporations. Their image in popular culture was of switches and blinking lights, emphasizing that first and foremost they were calculation machines—with no necessary relationship to optical media. In the era of the mainframe, the output of text and image was quite literally peripheral. Companies made a range of special-purpose devices to supplement mainframe computers that did not necessarily ship with screens or printers.

Stromberg-Carlson was one of these manufacturers. In 1954, the US Department of Defense contracted with it to supply a special-purpose mainframe peripheral for the SAGE (Semi-Automatic Ground Environment) computerized air defense system—a cathode ray tube (CRT) screen. SAGE was tricked out in firsts: among other things, it famously initiated the coordinated and systemic use of lightguns, duplexing, multiprocessing, modems, and computer networking over telephone lines. Nonetheless, the screen that functioned as a real-time graphical user interface is generally understood to be its most important feature. Manufactured by Stromberg-Carlson, it was the company's first flagship product, and the Defense Department order was its largest to date. The key dilemma for the SAGE designers was the need for highly legible text with a sufficiently rapid refresh rate to allow air force specialists to track aircraft in real time. Stromberg-Carlson engineered a CRT screen called the Charactron. Its shaped beam tube deflected electrons through a mask of alphanumeric characters, transferring these characters to the viewing area at very high resolution with a display rate of ten thousand characters per second.

In 1959, Stromberg-Carlson began manufacturing another mainframe peripheral based on the Charactron screen. This one did not offer real-time interactivity. The S-C 4020 microfilm recorder could be attached to the IBM 7090, 7094, 360, and other existing mainframes to present and preserve images and image sequences in ways that then-contemporary interactive computer screens simply could not. It could produce extraordinarily precise line drawings and text far above the level of pen-based plotters. It was a strange and elaborate apparatus with a tape drive for accepting instructions, a controlling buffer, a Charactron screen sealed in a light-tight compartment with a film camera and a photographic camera, and development equipment for these images. Because the S-C 4020 does not easily fit within linear genealogies of computing that move inexorably toward interactivity and real-time engagement, it has largely fallen "off the radar" of modern computer histories, despite its central importance as a peripheral for visualization for the mainframe computers of the late 1950s to the mid-1980s. Yet its use during that time was sufficiently widespread to prompt its own user group, its own conferences, and even its own specialized scientific journal. All told, the S-C 4020 produced the majority of the computer graphics of the late 1950s and early 1960s.

The Stromberg-Carlson Microfilm Recorder was not a cheap machine. It cost approximately $325,000 in the mid-1960s. The IBM 7094 to which it was it was frequently attached cost $3.5 million dollars. Running the S-C 4020 cost approximately $500 per minute of output.[1] The microfilm plotter's primary market was thus necessarily the same military agencies, research institutions, and corporations that purchased mainframe computers. S-C 4020 deliveries went to places like the University of California Radiation Laboratory, the Naval Ordnance Proving Ground, the Johns Hopkins University Operations Research Office (ORO), Eglin Air Force Base, and the Atlas Computer Laboratory in England. The S-C 4020 was an industrial technology that was widely used in a number of different contexts for more than fifteen years. In each of those contexts, it was upgraded and transformed in various ways. The Atlas lab, for example, has online documentation of some of the various camera upgrades and reconfigurations that took place between 1967 and 1972.

Such a complex history of technological reception and adaptation necessitates a delimited treatment. Thus, this study does not propose a wide-ranging treatment of the S-C 4020 and its relationship to the development of computer graphics across a sweeping international context. Rather, it focuses exclusively on the machine delivered to Bell Labs Research and Development in New Jersey. It does so not because of any inherent differences in the machine that was delivered there but rather because of the extraordinary uses to which it would be put between 1961 and 1972.

The machine purchased by Bell Laboratories was installed at its Murray Hill campus, an industrial lab in the suburban hills of New Jersey some twenty-five miles from the grit and noise of New York City. Surrounded by hundreds of acres of protected forest, scientists and engineers worked in brick and glass buildings while deer grazed on the lawns. Constructed in 1941, the campus was essentially one large building that housed around four thousand people engaged in a wide range of disciplinary research. The building had been designed to facilitate fortuitous and unexpected encounters. Offices and labs were intentionally small and separated into different corridors. Long hallways housed entire research divisions. Walking between corridors, in the atrium, and in the cafeteria, people encountered colleagues, digressions, and problems.

This intellectual ferment made Bell Labs home to some of the most significant breakthroughs in science and engineering from the 1920s to the 1980s. Transistors, lasers, satellites, cellular telephony, information theory: the list is long, and the story has been told many times.[2] Less well known is that in the 1960s, Bell Labs also became a crucial site in an epochal intersection between modern art, science, and technology as important as anything since the Bauhaus of the 1920s—and that a seemingly peripheral device, the S-C 4020 microfilm plotter, was at the heart of that intersection.

Bell Labs often enters the story of new media art via Experiments in Art and Technology (E.A.T.) with Robert Rauschenberg and Billy Klüver. With Experiments in Art and Technology, the artists are the driving, creative force; the engineers show up simply to implement their ideas. The rhetoric of the day emphasizes this: there were artists on one side, and engineers on the other, and their collaboration was the result of fortuitous encounters. Yet this binary is a drastic simplification if not an outright historical falsification, and it should not be allowed to persist. In the early work of Kenneth Knowlton and Michael Harmon, for instance, a coin was flipped to see who would be the engineer and who would be the artist—just one instance of how irrelevant these labels could be. And yet these labels cannot simply be ignored because they often had significant real-world implications—for how this work was made, where it was exhibited and encountered, and the discursive models through which it was discussed and conceptualized.

A close examination of the S-C 4020 and the work made with it leads us to another story, one that has been left out of the histories of that era. This story problematizes sites of exhibition, modes of work, and the collective role played by artists and engineers in producing both artistic advances and scientific innovations. Revealing a much closer overlap between art, science, and technology, this story shows how science and technology enable innovations in art practice, and how artistic practice also reshapes science and technology—transforming ideas about visual perception and innovation in computation.

Stromberg-Carlson advertised the S-C 4020 as offering the easy production of tabular data, graph plotting and design drawings, grid projections and drawing of axes and vectors, automatic forms projection, and permanent storage on microfilm. But the machine made all kinds of previously invisible objects and processes suddenly, startlingly visible—and made previously impossible visualizations remarkably possible. E. E. Zajac made the first computer film, simulating the motion of a communications satellite around the earth. Béla Julesz and Michael Noll made astonishing leaps in understanding depth perception in human vision by writing routines that created random-noise stereographs to answer questions about seeing that had gone unanswered since 1838. Kenneth Knowlton developed innovative techniques for scanning photographs, creating work collected by the Museum of Modern Art (MoMA) in New York. Stan VanDerBeek and Lillian Schwartz used Fortran-based computer languages to produce experimental cybernetic films generally regarded as crucial early works of computer art.

Because of the emphasis that Bell Labs placed on interdisciplinarity, artists were able to access equipment that was far more expensive than anything they could have afforded by themselves, and the presence of artists led scientists to think more expansively about their inquiries. In the history of computer visualization and computational media aesthetics, the importance of Bell Labs—and the work of Zajac, Noll, Knowlton, Harmon, VanDerBeek, Julesz, and Schwartz there—is canonical and established, though certainly not to the degree it deserves within histories of late modern art and aesthetics more generally. Yet what is insufficiently appreciated is the degree to which the work of these pioneers was influenced by the particular affordances of the S-C 4020 and the ways in which those affordances can help us to see important associations between these seemingly heterogeneous works. Literally as well as metaphorically, an acute attention to the peripheral allows us to understand the specific materiality and context of these interactions in ways that would not otherwise be possible.

Taking up the challenge of the Platform Studies series, *Peripheral Vision* provides a meticulous accounting of the hardware of the S-C 4020 that was used at Bell Labs—taking into account its configuration and architecture on the mutually interconnected level of software and hardware, as well as the culture of scientific research and military computing that drove its construction and initially framed its capabilities and possibilities.[3] In this, it works toward a materialist history of computation. It examines how software was developed for this platform and how this software was rewritten and reshaped to take better advantage of the hardware. *Peripheral Vision* considers how the unique technical affordances of this platform reshaped modes of scientific research and led to the creation of some of the most significant works of computer art in the 1960s. It also considers the widely divergent cultural contexts in which these images and films were shown and encountered. Secondarily, it emphasizes that there was not a direct, linear progression that moved ever more surely to personal, interactive computing. Instead, there was a significant period during the 1960s that was dominated by the mainframe computer and the possibilities of a mode of computation that was not based on direct access to a graphical user interface. In doing so, it develops an alternative genealogy of computer art at Bell Labs.

Looking closely at the S-C 4020 helps us to emphasize that computers are not singular machines, complete unto themselves, but complex, hybrid objects that are multiply layered and dependent on external systems. Using the S-C 4020 as an optic provides us with an indirect view of computer history that might serve to challenge some closely held methodological assumptions. Taking such a "peripheral" as our primary object might imply more than simply a rigorous attention to a set of concrete material technologies. It might also serve as a methodological appeal for a more oblique perspective on the history of technology more generally.

For while the mainframe computer has been universally acknowledged for shaping the evolution of graphics computation, the unsung S-C 4020 was just as significant to this history—precisely because of the specific limitations it imposed. Resituating "peripherals" as central to histories and theories of computation would demand that we attend to the historical materiality of particular computational systems not as they were intended at the outset but as they were adjusted and modified in actual practice. It highlights the necessity of considering partial elements, such as screens and disk drives, in any discussion of the "affordances" within any computational system. It emphasizes the need to situate these partial elements within increasingly larger systemic rings—computer systems but also political, social, and economic systems within which the material practices of computation acquire meaning and significance. And finally, it asks that we consider what it would entail to reconceptualize the writing of history—of both computer history and more general histories of technology and culture—from the perspective of this kind of "peripheral vision." This social-materialist model's oblique perspective might enable it to emphasize the key fault lines that inevitably persist beneath the surface of our familiar, overarching narratives.

With the Charactron screen, Stromberg-Carlson reshaped the field of computer graphics at a time when the mainframe computer was the rule rather than the exception. The Charactron was originally developed as a standalone screen, a peripheral whose most famous use was in the SAGE system. This chapter examines how the Charactron screen drew straight lines and curves from airplanes navigating the shifting currents and chaotic updrafts of the sky. With the Charactron, points were drawn and labeled, photographic clutter was reduced, and hardware and software combined to imagine a new model of visual perception.

Stromberg-Carlson later built this screen into a general-purpose graphic and text printing device—a machine for generating images that helped the computer "to talk in everyone's language," as their advertisements would have it.[1] The Stromberg-Carlson 4020 was what became known as a microfilm plotter—a peripheral device that combined several elements, including the Charactron cathode ray tube, a magnetic tape deck, a buffer unit, a forms flash unit, a film camera, and a photo-paper camera.

This chapter examines the relationship between computer and peripheral by carefully considering the process of programming the S-C 4020 as it was installed at Bell Labs in 1961. It was a complicated routine that involved Fortran, punchcards, an IBM 7094 mainframe, and magnetic tape reels. The chapter concludes with a close reading of the affordances of the S-C 4020 by looking at two examples that, like the screens of SAGE, combine language and vector "drawings"—E .E. Zajac's short film of a satellite orbiting the earth, typically credited as the first digital computer film ever made, and F. W. Sinden's Force, Mass and Motion, a depiction of Newton's Law using several different central force laws. The lines and curves of the films come from the Charactron screen, the jittery black and white from microfilm processing, and the complex physics from the IBM 7094's calculations. Shaped both by the Charactron's screen and a lingering cybernetic theory of vision and visuality, both works privilege the diagram over the photograph as a mode for producing knowledge by simulating the physicality of objects in the world.

As this chapter lays out, the S-C 4020 is a material collision of a number of different technologies, each with an individual history. The different technologies—magnetic tape, buffer, cathode ray tube, slide unit, cameras, and microfilm—came together in unexpected ways, and using the S-C 4020 required a careful negotiation of these complex affordances. In particular, the Charactron display's straight lines and easy-print characters had a massive effect on the development of the S-C 4020, but so too did its magnetic tape input, microfilm output, drivers, and logic boards, which functioned collectively to make up this complex apparatus.

A Special-Purpose Screen: The Charactron

Imagine, for a moment, that the year is 1958. You are a tracking operator in the air surveillance section of the US Air Force. Your job is to sit in a windowless room and watch a small round screen about sixteen inches in diameter, in a blue-lit room with other specialists stationed at identical screens, with different views. The scope in front of you refreshes itself in a steady clockwise sweep, displaying blips representing all of the air traffic in your sector, generated by long-range radar.

In your right hand is an object shaped like a backward pistol, with a sight on the top. It is attached by a connecting wire to the system you know as Semi-Automatic Ground Environment (SAGE). Within this computerized air defense system, individual moving objects—representing gathered data—are visually represented by small moving blips, which make their way across your screen. Each blip is understood as an object in motion. Aiming—firing—with your lightgun and sight, you select a specific blip on the radar screen, telling the computer to track that object.[2] Unidentifiable blips are immediately relayed to operators in the identification section, who are set to scramble planes to intercept enemy bombers.

This system is reminiscent of the analog computers used as gun controllers in a slightly earlier era. But SAGE was decked out with high-tech novelty: lightguns, duplexing, multiprocessing, modems, and computer networking over telephone lines were only some of its many innovations. Yet for the present discussion, its most important feature was unquestionably the screen that enabled a real-time graphical interface.

However, unlike earlier analog gun controllers, the SAGE system did not itself aim and fire. Rather, it was intended to deploy a squadron of bombers to perform this particular duty. Decisions—to launch planes, to fire missiles—had to be made quickly, by human operators. Thus, the interface for SAGE was straightforward, transparent. Or so *Life* magazine told its readers in 1957, saying that this enormous computer was able to summarize and present data "so clearly that the Air Force men who monitor SAGE can sit quietly in their weirdly lighted rooms watching its consoles and keep their minds free to make only the necessary human judgments of battle—when and where to fight."[3] The sky is an inherently shifting and chaotic space of unclarity—currents and updrafts, clouds and fog. For SAGE to work, the paths of objects and bodies within these spaces had to be rewritten into repeatable, replicable, easily transmissible curves and lines. Instrumentalizing vision, these machines required the human operator to accommodate himself to new paradigms of visualization.

Vision and perception are here reimagined arithmetically, while the human subject is reimagined as "manageable, predictable, productive, and above all consonant with other areas of rationalization."[4] These points are models rather than mimetic representations. This is an informatic relationship with the world. Alexander R. Galloway has recently suggested that "in order to be in a relation with the world informatically, one must erase the world, subjecting it to various forms of manipulation, preemption, modeling, and synthetic transformation."[5] The screens abstract to essentials, reducing visual clutter in favor of structural understanding. These images construct a complex yet structurally integrated system—a dynamic interrelation of elements. Above all, this screen insisted that its abstract vectors and symbols bore an indexical relationship to the world—a truth claim most commonly held to be confined to the domain of the photographic. The dream here is of a vision that might employ automation to permit "rapid, accurate, and detailed central oversight."[6] And "oversight," in this context, is not a term present by happenstance. The becoming-pictorial of computers would be intimately intertwined with a military imperative for command and control, with visual mastery, and as such, with what psychoanalytic philosophy would call the "scopic drive."

As late as 1947, officers of the air staff thought that the kind of surveillance represented by the SAGE project was impossible and that there was no way for the air force to continually monitor the skies over the entire United States for hostile bombers. Full coverage radar, combining electronic monitoring with human observers, was impractical. Worse, it was potentially disastrous, as it left "little room for the air offensive," which was seen as the only hope for real security.[7] The 1947 Air Policy

Commission, assigned by President Harry Truman, also opposed a full-coverage radar system using a similar rationale, arguing it would "divert us—as the Maginot Line diverted France—from the best defense against an atomic attack, the counter-offensive string force" already in place.[8] Calculations changed in 1949, when the Russians detonated an atomic bomb several years ahead of the timetable projected by US intelligence. The cold war escalated precipitously, and Congress granted emergency war powers. Budgets abruptly increased, money flowed like water, and suddenly, a technologically updated Maginot line of integrated radar units that could oversee the skies became a priority for the Defense Department and the National Security Council.

The air force found the technical beginnings for this project in the Whirlwind system, a Massachusetts Institute of Technology project originally built as a flight simulator and subsequently reimagined as an anti-aircraft computer. But as engineers and programmers labored to develop SAGE from this framework, they realized that Whirlwind lacked something crucial—a means of interactive control. It had a screen, but as developer Norman H. Taylor stated, "All we used the display for was testing the various parts of the system."[9] SAGE needed "a man-machine interactive display system to exercise control."[10] Not only did it need screens—it needed a lot of them, enough "to control over 400 aircraft simultaneously. [The original] estimate of 32 consoles grew to 64 and then to 82."[11] And those displays certainly had to be "a little more sophisticated than a point of light on a cathode ray tube."[12]

George Valley, one of the heads of the SAGE project, pointed out that in the 1950s, "relatively few wanted to connect computers to the real world, and these people seemed to believe that the sensory devices would all yield data.... Most sensory devices relied on human operators to interpret noisy and complex signals."[13] Two Stromberg-Carlson employees confirmed this in an article on the screen that they manufactured for SAGE and other applications: "not too long ago in surveillance systems, it was sufficient to present raw radar and supplementary data to observers. The systems performed satisfactorily, since the observer had sufficient time to calculate the necessary information for his task manually from the raw data."[14] But in the present, "it is becoming increasingly important to provide the observer with sufficient quantity and quality of information to make decisions more accurately and rapidly. The problem is being continually magnified because of the increased speed and number of objects under surveillance. As a result, raw radar data and manual calculation are no longer adequate."[15] As a result of this, Stromberg-Carlson was working to link the electronic data-processing equipment directly with character-generating cathode ray tubes: "The data processing equipment converts the raw data into digital form, after which it is presented to the observer as letters, numbers, and symbols by the cathode ray tube."[16]

SAGE's computers and screens needed to make noisy and complex signals clear and legible to a human operator. They needed a display that could draw vectors and characters and assemble these elements into orderly message patterns to allow the air force specialists to track airplanes in real time.[17] And it needed this display to have a rapid refresh rate. The solution they found was the Charactron, a special-purpose cathode ray tube that was invented by Joseph T. McNaney for computer readout, high-speed printing, high-speed communications, monitoring, and message display.[18]

The base of the Charactron was the same basic cathode ray tube that was used in televisions and oscilloscopes. Although displaced by flatscreen technology at the beginning of the millenium, the venerable cathode ray tube served as the basis for countless televisions and computer monitors in the second half of the twentieth century. It consisted of a vacuum tube that contains an electron gun (an electron-emitting filament and a control grid), control elements that regulate where the electron beam hits the screen, and a phosphor-coated screen that renders the strike of the electron beam as visible light. The Charactron added something generally called shaped-beam technology to this.

Prior to the Charactron, shaped beam had been used primarily to transmit images rather than as a sort of printing press. As early as 1937, "monotron" CRT screens were made by companies such as National Union and Du Mont.[19] RCA produced a similar tube in 1945, called the "monoscope." Monoscopes were special-purpose CRT tubes equipped with a target printed with a pattern. When the target was scanned with an electron beam, it interrupted the current flow, creating a picture signal that matched the printed pattern.[20] The screen could produce only black and white, but gray could be simulated with delicate lines or newspaper-style halftone dots. RCA's monoscopes were used primarily for fairly intricate television test patterns—the patterns broadcast during a television station's downtime. The monoscope can be understood as a predecessor to the Charactron, but it was designed to display a single image rather than a combination of text and graphics.

Like the monoscope, the Charactron shaped-beam tube adds another element to a simple CRT tube—a metal stencil, generally called a *matrix*, located between the electron gun and the phospor screen. The stencil is tiny, with up to sixty-four characters taking up less than a quarter inch of space. Precisely angled deflection plates guide the beam to a particular area of the stencil. Where the electron beam hits the solid metal of the stencil, it stops. But the portion of the beam that hits the open area passes through and takes on the shape of the stencil. When this "shaped beam" hits the phosphor screen, the visible light is shaped and then positioned on the screen by additional deflection plates. This can produce a sharp, clear image of any number of special characters, in addition to regular alphanumeric symbols. Anything that can be cut into a stencil can be precisely displayed on the screen. After the characters appear on the screen, they can be read or photographed.[21] Because the tube deflected electrons through a mask of alphanumeric characters (transferring the characters at very high resolution to the viewing area rather than tracing the characters onscreen with the beam itself), it meant that a high rate of speed was possible: characters could be displayed at a rate of ten thousand per second. This was a crucial evolution in graphics—but also a stopgap, generated from necessity. Nevertheless, this technology left its mark on the history of computer graphics.

Stromberg-Carlson built the Charactron shaped-beam tube into a hybrid apparatus called the S-C 4020 that consisted of a seven-inch Charactron shaped-beam tube "associated electronic controls and logical circuitry," an automatic operated camera (also controlled by the system), and an input device that utilized magnetic tape.[22] This device, as a whole, was variously called a *microfilm plotter*, a *microfilm printer*, a *microfilm recorder*, or a *computer-operated microfilm (COM)* device. The first term links it to the mechanical analog plotter that was used as an output device for mainframe

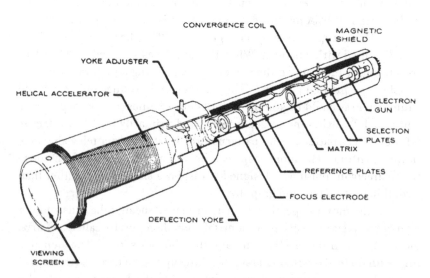

Charactron tube diagram from a Stromberg-Carlson advertisement.

computers both prior to and after the development of the microfilm plotter. Through digital to analog conversion, the mechanical plotter takes signals from a computer and uses them to direct an armlike machine that draws pencil or pen lines on flat paper or drum carriages of paper. They made precise drawings but were not particularly fast. They were used to make films by means of steady animation but were primarily for producing two-dimensional images on paper. The second term, *printer*, links it to the devices attached to computers to print text, line by line. They were fast but not particularly amenable to graphics. *Microfilm recorder* draws an analogy to either a film or tape recorder and emphasizes the durational nature of the media output. *COM* highlights the computerized aspect of the device. It was also sometimes called a *computer recorder*, further highlighting the hybridity of the apparatus. These terms were often used interchangeably in referring to the device and in advertising it. This speaks in part to a device with widespread use whose use was nonetheless in flux and transition. I have chosen in this text to call the S-C 4020 a microfilm plotter. It is not necessarily the most widely used nomenclature, but it is roughly on par with the term microfilm recorder, and it speaks to both the strangeness of the device and its intimate relationship with prior analog apparatuses used for both input and output.

As would be expected, Stromberg-Carlson and then Stromberg-Datagraphix produced training guides for the operators and technicians who would be responsible for using and repairing the machines. The training guides described how to troubleshoot particular technologies, but somewhat unexpectedly, they also explained the historical background for the device. Three particular elements were singled out—the CRT screen (as has been discussed), magnetic tape, and microfilm processing.[23]

High-Speed Input: Magnetic Tape

Magnetic tape recording devices were initially used in computer systems in 1951 as a replacement of sorts for punchcards.[24] Although crucial for computer development, magnetic tape was a nineteenth-century technology. Danish engineer Valdemar Poulsen successfully experimented with magnetic wire in 1898, creating his "telegraphone," a machine that connected a strung-out steel piano wire and an electromagnet to a microphone. Poulson ran the electromagnet over the wire while talking into the microphone and then played back the recording by connecting the wires from the magnet to a telephone receiver.[25] Recorders with steel tapes were made in Germany in the 1920s, and in 1935, a machine with a plastic base and a magnetic coating was exhibited in Berlin. After that point, the technology developed rapidly, with audio and video applications, and following World War II, data storage.

Paul Ceruzzi calls the rows and rows of spinning magnetic tape reels "the true characteristic of the mainframe," pointing out that "the popular image of these devices was that of 'giant brains,' mainly because of the tapes' uncanny ability to run in one direction, stop, read or write some data, then back up, stop again, and so on, all without human intervention."[26] High-speed computers needed high-speed data to take advantage of the capacities of the machine: "The speed of the automatic computer system is derived primarily from the stored-program concept wherein both the program and the information to be operated upon are contained within the Memory Section."[27]

Memory was fantastically expensive at this point, and magnetic tape served as an "auxiliary memory": it stored information that could then be read and placed in the main memory. Although not as fast as later magnetic disk storage, which offered random access, magnetic tape was still comparatively fast and offered substantial amounts of sequential storage at a time when this was highly desirable. A magnetic tape reader was able to transfer data quickly and easily into the main computer memory.[28]

Or in the case of the S-C 4020, it could transfer data *out* of the main computer memory. As Frank Dietrich points out, "in contrast with today's frame buffers, which hold the image memory in their bit map," the S-C 4020's images "resided in the computer's main memory."[29] More precisely, the image was held in the reel of magnetic tape that was exported from the mainframe computer. Later versions of the peripheral, including the 4060, included a stored program unit, but the 4020 read directly from the magnetic tape.[30] The display driver takes the input from the tape and displays the desired lines and characters on the Charactron. As would be expected, the S-C 4020 understood a limited range of commands. The magnetic tape could carry commands that drew on the screen, including PLOT, EXPOSE LIGHT, EXPOSE HEAVY, TYPE SPECIFIED POINT, TYPE CURRENT POINT, DRAW VECTOR, GENERATE X-AXIS, GENERATE Y-AXIS, and PROJECT FORM. Other commands (SELECT CAMERA 2, SELECT BOTB CAMERAS, EXPAND IMAGE, REDUCE IMAGE, ADVANCE FILM, and PROJECT FORM) controlled camera selection and movement and also allowed for the projection of a blank form template superimposed on the screen.

The vector generator could connect two addressable points with a straight line to produce a geometric graph. The variable-length generator was able to draw a continuous vertical or horizontal line extending the full length or width of the frame, beginning at any plotting position. This added two types of straight-line vector generation to the character matrix. Characters could be positioned by selecting one of 1,024 horizontal positions with one of 1,024 vertical positions. In the normal printing mode, a frame of film could record 64 lines with up to 128 characters on each line; when developed, this translated to a page of output. There was also a typewriter simulator that eliminated the need to generate position data for each character by placing characters automatically on a horizontal line and returning to the "margin" to create a new line when a line was finished.

This narrow range of instructions was nevertheless able to produce fairly complex images quite quickly. An ad for Stromberg-Carlson promoted the speed of the S-C 4020, stating that that it

> will accept data from magnetic tape at input rates up to 62,500 six-bit characters per second. It will record this data on film at speeds in excess of 17,000 alphanumeric or symbolic characters per second. Frames combining characters, vectors and curves vary with the complexity of the specific drawing, but an average annotated graph can be recorded by the S-C 4020 in less than a second.[31]

Information was transferred from tape to the S-C 4020 with a 36-bit input register. The control unit breaks each 36-bit word into its two essential pieces—the operation code and the information (such as specific screen position, character code, or stopping point) that is required to complete the specified operation.[32]

The Output: Microfilm

The S-C 4020 output to microfilm, a nineteenth-century technology that made photography microscopic, allowing for what originally seemed to be an infinite storage capacity. "The whole archives of a nation might be packed away in a small snuff box," opined an optimistic writer for *Photographic News* in 1859: "Had the art been known in the time of Omar, the destruction of the Alexandrian Library would not have been a total loss."[33] Microfilm was thus originally imagined as a hedge against loss, a means of ceaselessly expanding storage capacity that could bypass the fickle nature of paper, which was prone to disintegration and destruction:

> Let us imagine the number of wills or mortgages liable to be destroyed, which would cause boundless litigation.... A microscopic negative of which, carefully stored away ... would give a document as reliable as the original. Hundreds of thousands of such negatives might be put

away to be resuscitated upon the loss of the objects from which they were taken.... I trust that it will be the custom to make microscopic negatives of all valuable public documents.[34]

The microfilm industry began in 1839 with English scientist John Benjamin Dancer, who sold images that had to be examined with a microscope. A technique for making these miniature images was patented in France by René Dagron in 1859. But microfilm became an industrial technology in 1870 during the Franco-Prussian War when it became an answer to the problem of communication over enemy lines. In September 1870, Paris was surrounded by the Prussians and cut off from the rest of France. Telegraph lines were slashed. Mail service was halted. The provincial government in Tours struggled to establish reliable communication with Paris. Sheepdogs failed to traverse enemy lines. Lightweight zinc balls, packed with messages, sunk in the Seine. Balloons transported millions of letters from the city, but return service by the same method was capricious and erratic. The idea they hit upon, finally, was an archaic one—the pigeon. But these were special pigeons, armed with the latest technology.

The Pigeon Post, as it was called, was a startling convergence of multiple technologies and interests. Racing pigeon enthusiasts, balloonists, photographers, and chemists pulled together to create a fairly robust communication network. The pigeons were airlifted out of Paris by balloon to ensure their escape over the Prussian lines. On their return journey, each pigeon carried messages placed in tiny tubes, and tightly attached to the pigeon's feathers. The initial trials used thin paper and handwritten messages, but there were weight and space limits, as well as lapses in penmanship. Microfilm became the linchpin for a national communication system. René Dagron was named the "chef de service des correspondances postales photomicroscopiques." He and his associates were sent to Tours and then Bordeaux, and the microfilm-equipped pigeon dispatch service quickly became operational.[35] In contrast to the handwritten messages, microfilm was extremely light in weight, so a pigeon could carry up to twenty in a small tube.[36] The loaded pigeon flew over the German lines and arrived at a Parisian loft. A bell rang, and the pigeon relinquished its tube to a handler, who transferred it to the Central Telegraph Office. There, each individual microfilm sheet was placed between glass and illuminated via magic lantern. Clerks transcribed the messages for delivery on telegraph forms, taking care to affix a special annotation—"pigeon."[37] But "microfilm" would have been an equally appropriate marker for the 2.5 million messages transmitted.

Over the next seventy years, microfilm took on increasing importance in industry and research. Microfilm began to be used in the financial industry with the development of a machine that made copies of canceled checks for permanent storage by banks. The Library of Congress began to use it as an archival material and microfilmed books and manuscripts. During World War II, it was used to safeguard engineering drawings. With the destruction of cultural artifacts and monuments, war also brought home the need to preserve archives, collections, and cultural documents, and the end of the war saw an uptick in archival preservation using microfilm records.

Despite its original purpose as still imagery, by the 1960s, microfilm unexpectedly became a crucial element in computer motion graphics. Microfilm plotters such as the S-C 4020 were, in effect, self-contained systems for film recording, usable by a range of scientists and engineers who did not necessarily have any prior experience—or even interest—in movie making. As Gene Youngblood wrote in 1970, "users of microfilm plotters have found ... that their movie-producing capability is at least as valuable as their storage-and-retrieval capability."[38] As such, they quickly became the most utilized output system for the nascent idea of the computer film.

Synthetic Cinematography

A film made by E. E. Zajac on the S-C 4020 is often referred to as the first computer graphics film.[39] It was Zajac's first film, as well, as he was not a filmmaker by either trade or initial inclination. The film is disarmingly simple. A box, drawn in sharp white lines against a black background, slowly tumbles around a gridded sphere, with a dial in the corner counting off the rotations. Partway through, the view switches to focus on the box, which wobbles side to side before gradually stabilizing. It is not an exciting film, but it is sharply evocative of a new paradigm of visualization. The clean lines articulate a system that hews to clear-cut laws and rhythms independent of cinematic observation. The view is of a control and relay system floating around an earth that had only recently been visualized from space, though never from that particular angle. This view could have been hand-drawn in the past, but the precise mathematical rigor of the depiction is new.

The rigor develops because Zajac was not initially interested in computer graphics or animation, per se. Only after writing about the film did he become interested in the possibilities that the microfilm plotter and computer offered for scientific visualization more generally. The film,

Simulation of a Two-Gyro Gravity-Gradient Attitude Control System, was made because Zajac was interested in real-time modeling of an attitude-control system for an orbiting communication satellite. The abstraction of the film is in part because Zajac was not developing a specific attitude-control system but rather working on developing "general guiding principles and analytic and numerical techniques useful in such a design program."[40]

When Zajac was working on this in the early 1960s, the satellite business was relatively new, and the space above the earth was not yet cluttered

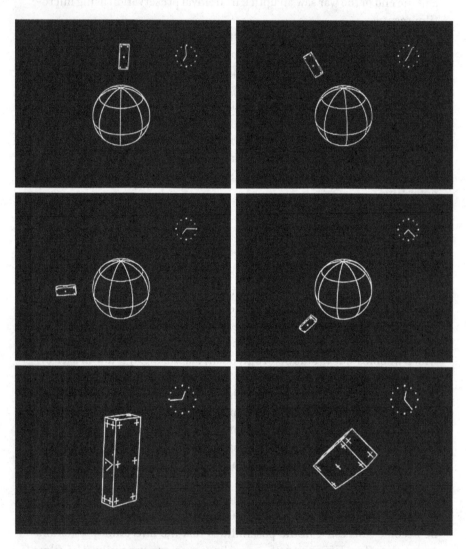

Stills from E. E. Zajac's film *Simulation of a Two-Gyro Gravity-Gradient Attitude Control System* (1963).

with man-made detritus. Bell Labs, in conjunction with the National Aeronautics and Space Administration (NASA), had made an initial foray into space in 1960 with something that it called *Echo* and most people called a "satelloon"—an inflatable satellite described retrospectively as "perhaps the most beautiful object ever to be put into space."[41] Launched in the aftermath of the Russians' 1957 *Sputnik 1*, *Echo 1* was designed not just to enable visual and auditory communication but to be seen and talked about—a man-made American satellite that amateur astronomers could track with telescopes, that would hover in the sky as a signal of American ingenuity and technical know-how. *Echo 1* was a dazzling, highly reflective sphere with a 100-foot diameter and a 31,416 square foot surface of Mylar polyester film covered smoothly with vapor-deposited aluminum. As its name suggested, it was a passive satellite, a surface that could angle a precisely directed signal from, say, California down to New Jersey. Unfortunately, its shape made it a weak passive reflector: it was able to distribute a signal fairly broadly but unable to focus it.

A follow-up project, *Telstar 1*, was far smaller—only 34.5 inches in diameter. It was less aesthetically noteworthy but was substantially more effective at signal broadcast mechanics. As the first active communications satellite, *Telstar* did not just reflect signals but amplified and retransmitted them. Moreover, these signals were not confined to radio transmissions but could be telephone calls, images, or television feeds. *Telstar* was launched on July 10, 1962, at 4:35 in the morning. Later that day, the first television picture—of a waving American flag in Andover, Maine—was transmitted via satellite, marking and laying claim to a new terrain of communication.

Zajac was part of a group working on research and development for a successor to *Telstar 1*.[42] His subgroup was studying the orientation control of satellites.[43] *Telstar* was able to stabilize itself such that during its orbit, one face of the satellite always pointed to earth. But *Telstar* had been an experiment, and Zajac was working on guiding principles for a next-generation stabilization system. He states that "at first, I had the computer print out numbers giving the satellite orientation at successive instants of time. The problem of visualizing the satellite motions from the printed numbers was formidable."[44] Instead, Zajac "wrote a subprogramme which took the numbers that would normally be printed out and used them to compute a perspective drawing of a box representing a satellite."[45] According to Zajac, this had a number of advantages: graphical output was "'natural' ... The human eye has great pattern recognition ability: for this very reason the usual first step in handling scientific data is to plot it."[46]

The film was divided into two parts. The first part shows the motion of the satellite around the earth. The switch to a view of just the satellite displays the gyro stabilization but also reveals a striking possibility of computer-generated films—the rapid transformation of perspective. Because the essence of the computer film lies in a numerical input rather than the optical registrations of a physical camera, sudden and dramatic changes in viewpoint could be achieved quite easily.[47]

This 1963 film represents a system—an increasingly pervasive concern for filmmakers who were interested in, as Gene Youngblood put it, "systems aesthetics, scientific discipline, and so on."[48] But Zajac was not a filmmaker. And as Youngblood pointed out, "most computer films are not aesthetically motivated. They are made by scientists, engineers, and educators to facilitate visualization and rapid assimilation of complex analytic and abstract concepts."[49] Zajac's film simulated the motion of a communications satellite around the earth.[50] This simulation was the result of numerical integration of differential equations. The results were depicted as perspectival drawings, giving visual form to a mathematical system in a way that would have been nearly impossible before the advent of the computer. Looking back at 1960s computing, Melvin Pruitt has written,

> the results of computer simulations were printed out on large stacks of paper. The results were numbers. The main problem was that when we looked at page 15 and saw hundreds of numbers, then turned over to page 250 and saw thousands of other numbers, how could we see the relationship between numbers on so many different pages?[51]

Interpreting them was difficult if not impossible. Zajac's film offered a different way of dealing with those hundreds of numbers.

Zajac saw those numbers and their manipulation as the crucial element of his film. He argued that "the advantages of computer animation do not lie with an elaborately versatile cathode ray tube. Rather they lie with the power of a high speed digital computer. Indeed, the special virtue of computer animation is that it brings the power of computing to the film medium."[52] Previously, he pointed out, these kinds of films had to be elaborately drawn by hand, with all of the calculations done by an animator. Although the computer was a crucial part of this operation, the microfilm plotter was clearly just as important. For with the advent of computer output microfilm, the computer could perform the calculations while the microfilm plotter functioned as draftsman—but the limitations and constraints of this apparatus were largely on the side of the S-C 4020.

Programming a Film

The computer that was performing these calculations was a mainframe, a beast of a computer utterly unlike the laptops and desktops that we associate with the term today. The S-C 4020 was used at Bell Labs primarily as a peripheral for the IBM 7090 and 7094 computers. The IBM 7090 filled a room to overflowing and generated an extraordinary amount of noise. Not only was the room noisy, but it was freezing in an attempt to cope with the seemingly endless amount of heat generated by the machine. The 7094 was an upgrade of the IBM 7090, quite literally: a company could purchase a few components to transform its 7090 into a 7094.

If you have seen a mainframe in a Hollywood film, chances are excellent it was a 7094, which, for a time, must have seemed like the platonic ideal of "the computer." It had dials, gauges, switches, and blinking lights. The lights showed the status of the computer's registers, bit by bit. They let the operator read each register in the central processor directly, in binary numbers, in case of glitches or errors. The operator could execute a program one instruction at a time, watching the registers intently. The switches allowed operators to alter the bits on particular registers, giving operators a high level of control over the machine on an exceedingly fine-grained level.[53]

The 7090 was a transistorized computer introduced in 1959, only a year after IBM had begun deliveries of the 709, a vacuum-tube–based computer. The 7090 was architecturally identical to the 709, but it substituted transistors for the suddenly obsolete vacuum tubes. The key reason for the substitution was the US Air Force. IBM bid on an air force contract for a follow-up to the Semi-Automatic Ground Environment (SAGE) air defense system, intending to offer the vacuum-tube–based 709, but the air force was interested only in a transistorized computer.[54] IBM won the contract with the 7090, which maintained the essential architecture of the 709 but used the newer transistor technology. The 7094 was simply an upgrade of the initial system, and functioned very similarly.

According to Paul Ceruzzi, the 7090/7094 "is regarded as the classic mainframe because of its combination of architecture, performance and financial success: hundreds of machines were installed at a price of around $2 million each."[55] It was designed for large-scale scientific and technical operations. It had a flexible design, intended to "ease maintenance and accessibility."[56] Each cabinet had modular sliding frames with two vertical racks that could be pulled from the frame and opened to access the hundreds of transistor cards it contained. The computer is made up of standardized modules to enable easy accessibility and maintenance. Each of the units has two vertical drawers that pull out to reveal two hinged "pages." When these pages are closed, the wiring is exposed, which allows access to all text points. When pulled to an open position, the pluggable printed wiring transistor cards are simple to remove and replace. Modularization is intended to enable efficiency. A typical installation involved a number of these standardized cabinets mounted a few inches over a tiled floor, leaving space for thick cables that connected one cabinet to another.

The IBM 7090 was six times faster than the 709, which IBM attributed to more than fifty thousand transistors coupled with exceptionally fast magnetic core storage. The system was capable of reading and writing electronically at a rate of three million bits of information a second: "In 2.18 millionths of a second, it can locate and make ready for use any of 32,768 data or instruction numbers (each of 10 digits) in the magnetic core storage. The 7090 can perform any of the following operations in one second: 229,000 additions or subtractions, 39,500 multiplications, or 32,700 divisions."[57]

The 7090 was a custom built system, tailored to user specifications. There were some strictly necessary components —a card reader, a printer, a console control unit, core storage, a central processing unit, a multiplexor, a data channel, and a power convertor. But there were other optional elements: a card puncher, two magnetic tape units, and two types of data channels (tape or tape with card), as well as various third-party peripherals. A fully tricked out IBM 7090 system could include eighty magnetic tape units, eight card readers, eight card punches, and eight printers. The product announcement package stated that the system was designed for use with real-time input and output. This "real-time" was highly relative, however. While its speed was leaps and bounds ahead of its predecessors, it was still a far cry from the interactive computing that now is understood as real-time.

The computer was too expensive to ever remain idle; it was always running programs on tape. This mode of programming was called "batch mode": one program was loaded and run at a time. The programmer never had direct access to the machine but had to wait for the results when the program was run. If there was a problem, a new deck had to be submitted and rerun. In the early 1960s, computing at Bell Labs was done primarily on a 7090 or 7094 system in batch mode. Programmers rarely encountered the machine itself. They worked on decks of punched cards. Some programmers did not even keypunch the cards themselves but wrote out sets of instructions on "coding sheets" (a phrase that gives rise to our current reference to computer programming as coding) that were given to keypunch operators to create the cards. An IBM 1401—a small special purpose computer—translated the cards into rolls of magnetic tape.

As noted earlier, magnetic tape drives governed the mainframe. Tapes were the intermediary between the computer, its programmers, and its peripherals. An operator took the tape from the 1401 and loaded it into the IBM 7090. The operator's job was to mount and demount tapes, set switches and punch buttons to put a job into motion, check the flashing lights for occasional problems, and attend to status information printouts. Ceruzzi reminds us that while a few mainframes had video consoles, the 7094 was not one of them, and "such a console would have been useful only for control purposes, since the sequential storage on tapes prevented direct access to data anyway."[58] Video consoles were not generally employed due to their "voracious appetite for core memory."[59]

Peripherals like the S-C 4020 took on an outsized importance because they were the only source of visual display for the mainframe computer. As noted earlier, Zajac argues that the peripheral is not as important for computer animation as the computer connected to it. And from the perspective of the future development of computer animation, his point is well taken. Nevertheless, the composition of Zajac's own film was dictated—far more than he was willing to admit—by the affordances specific to the peripheral. To explain this importance, it is helpful to detail the actual process of programming a film as Zajac presented it in his 1966 article for *New Scientist*.

In this article, Zajac examines how the program for an animated film was written. He starts with a basic line drawing command: "CALL LINE (-5, 3, 15, 22)." This command tells the display device to draw a line between $X = -5$, $Y = 3$ and $X = 15$, $Y = 22$. As Zajac points out, this command is written in Fortran (Formula Translation), which was then a widely used scientific programming language. One of the advantages of Fortran was that its syntax—the set of rules that defines the how symbols are combined—was akin to ordinary algebra and thus familiar to the average scientist or engineer.[60]

With only two simple commands—

```
Y=5

CALL LINE (-15,Y,30,Y)
```

—the programmer can tell the computer to draw a horizontal from the point $X = -15$, $Y = 5$ to $X = 30$, $Y = 5$. A few more commands allow the computer to set up a loop:

```
DO THRU*, I = 1,100
```

```
Y=1

*CALL LINE (-15,Y,30,Y)
```

The DO THRU line sets the loop in process and tells the computer to run the following instructions (up to and including the instruction marked by the asterisk) 100 times: "Each time through the loop, the Y coordinate of the line is given the value of the counter, I. So on the 29th pass through the loop Y = 29, on the 30th pass Y = 30."[61] Zajac's example here directs the computer to draw a hundred parallel lines, each spaced a single unit apart.

These instructions could be used to create an animated film because of some specific attributes of the S-C 4020. The cameras in microfilm plotters did not work like standard cinema cameras. In cinema cameras, the shutter was an integrated part of the camera that was mechanically linked with the film advance function. In microfilm plotters, the computer controlled the shutter and could operate that shutter independently from the film advance mechanism. In practice, this meant a single frame could be held open for as long as it took the CRT to draw a picture—or it could be advanced as quickly as the CRT tube could draw.

Zajac explains this by introducing the instruction "CALL FRAME" to his sample Fortran program. Fortran translates this to a command to the S-C 4020, which tells it to advance the film by one frame. The program now reads as follows:

```
DO THRU*, I = 1,100

Y=1

CALL LINE (-15,Y,30,Y)

*CALL FRAME
```

And with this addition, the S-C 4020 produces a 100-frame animated film instead of a single image. Zajac stresses that there are several points to be made here. First, a computer loop differs in kind from a film loop. A film loop hinges on identical repetition. A computer loop is based on repetition with a prescribed difference. Although it repeats a sequence of commands over and over, "a command, such as Y = I, may call for a change from the previous passage through the loop. Thus the event produced in each passage through the loop generally *differs in a systematic way* from the event produced in the previous passage."[62] Second, Zajac also points out the ease of changing this program to produce a new, different animation. A change in the value of Y from 1 to 1/2, for instance, would make the film last twice as long.[63] Changing the values of X changes the length of the line.

This means that a single basic program can generate far more than a single film: "it makes possible a whole *family* of films."[64] Finally, this program can be stored as a subroutine and called up as necessary as a part of a film.

Zajac's film was made possible, in part, by the creation of such a subroutine by F. W. Sinden, who wrote a program that calculated the orbits of massive bodies under central force action. Sinden used this to create a film that, following Zajac's argument, we can see as one of a family of films related to Zajac's. Called *Force, Mass and Motion*, it looks, as might be expected, very similar to Zajac's. But Zajac's work was only incidentally a film. More fundamentally, it was an experiment in stabilization—one that had proven difficult to simulate in the laboratory but simple to calculate with a computer. That the visualization thus produced took the form of a film was something of a happy accident. Sinden, by contrast, had specifically set out to make an educational film—one that would illustrate Newton's basic laws within a two-dimensional format: "Orbits are shown of two massive bodies under central force action for various laws, such as inverse cube, direct cube, etc., as well as for the familiar inverse square law."[65]

Like Zajac's film, Sinden's appears straightforward—white circles on a black background, straight lines, dots and arrows indicating trajectories. It has a bit of the pervasive registration jitter that accompanies all of the early films made with the S-C 4020. It is comprised entirely of dots and straight-line segments. It is divided into several sections, showing the motion of two gravitating bodies under a variety of circumstances, examining what the motion of bodies might look like if the law of gravity were very different:

> Most of the sequences in this film were made by a single programme of some sixty instructions together with a dozen or so named subprogrammes of five or ten instructions each. The latter performed such services as drawing circles, drawing arrows, specifying the law of attraction and controlling sweeps and zooms of an imaginary camera. Only the initial data and the subprogrammes varied from sequence to sequence, yet *visually* the sequences are quite different. This is typical for computer films demonstrating scientific principles. The basic programme defines a general law of nature (in this case, Newton's law of acceleration) while the different sequences show concrete manifestations of the law.[66]

Agreeing with Zajac, Sinden claims that "although the recent availability of precise, automatic microfilm recorders deserves credit for making computer-animation technically possible, the real secret behind it, as behind most computer applications, lies with the powerful techniques of computer programming that have been developed over the last decade and a half."[67] It is doubtless correct to give advances in programming the chief credit for the production of the data that underlie these animations. Yet if these data sets were to be visualized, the terms of that visualization would be given by the particular affordances and restrictions inherent to the S-C 4020 platform.

In drawing a picture, the computer gives a precise location "a horizontal and vertical co-ordinate—for each dot and for the end-points of each line-segment. Thus, pictures of any complexity, especially if they contain curves, require considerable data."[68] The resolution of the image is limited by the width of the electron beam and the specific raster layout of the screen: "The bright dot produced by the electron beam can be positioned only at points of the raster. Thus every dot in the picture must be centered on a raster point and every line segment must join raster points."[69] Sinden claims that this is not so much a restriction as the very condition of possibility for digital filmmaking: "in a digital machine, locations on the face of the tube must be specified by numbers of finite precision, and number of finite precision can specify only a finite set of locations."[70] He contends that under these restrictions, "the easiest and most natural subjects for a computer to animate are those in which both the drawings and the motion are easily specified by mathematical formulae. This means, above all, pictures representing physical and mathematical phenomena."[71] Zajac's film and Sinden's share some crucial assumptions about representation that were aided and abetted by the specific mechanical limitations of the S-C 4020. Crucially, neither of them displayed images that appeared anything like real objects in the world. They were not intended to mimic photographic representation of objects but rather to offer an abstract, *diagrammatic* representation of the systems within which objects were embedded. A traditional film might show a particular example of gravity as it would appear to humans in the real world—an apple falling from a tree, for instance. These films use vector drawings to sidestep the incidental detail of any given physical example.

The operative mechanics of these films? First, the reduction of objects to a schematic outline. Second, the division of the whole into parts for the purpose of recombination. The films are repeatedly referenced not as complete works but as constellations of relational elements. Read through the Fortran programs and the iterability possible with the microfilm plotter, these works do not exist as a stable representations but as ones explicitly designed for mutability. Their value is not their mimetic qualities but rather the ways in which they modeled certain functional and dynamic relationships.

Although revolutionary and powerful, the vector display brought with it certain assumptions regarding the nature of representation and visualization. It was able to present beautiful, clearly defined lines and curves but was troubled by shading and gradations. Practices of photographic and photorealistic representation more akin to human perception remained largely untenable, alien to its logic, and unable to be integrated into its visual system. Crisp and clean in black and white, the films were drawings comprised of simple line segments. Unlike Roland Barthes's description of the photograph—the basis of traditional filmic representation—they did not represent a "message without a code."[72] In fact, to the untrained eye, they would not have looked like much of anything in particular.

The twentieth century belongs, in most accounts, to the photograph—both as a system of representation and as a transformative social phenomenon. These films, in contrast, could more accurately be described as diagrams. The diagram is an older mode of representation—one tied to engineering and architecture, geometry, mathematics, and physics, among other disciplines and practices—that took on a new urgency in the rise of a culture of computation.[73] As with photography, there are various histories of diagrams. In his research on the technical drawing, Wolfgang Lefevre argues that the diagram emerges simultaneously with the figure of the engineer as a result of reorganizations in technology and production that demanded the combination of practical and scientific knowledge—a combination of action and understanding.[74]

Gilles Châtelet claims that the diagram has historically been considered "a subsidiary tool for representing equations."[75] Yet the diagram, as he describes it, serves a similar function in mathematics as in other disciplines: it "does not simply illustrate or translate an already available content. The diagrams are ... concerned with experience."[76] According to Châtelet, the diagram does not predict or verify a law but exists as a thought experiment: "If it is 'ideal' or 'theoretical,' it is not because it is impossible to carry out with 'real' instruments, but because it claims to question or uncover processes of idealization."[77] In other words, the diagram both questions and uncovers the process by which ideals are formed in the mind.

Anthony Vidler, for example, has recently explored the history of the diagram as a means of response to its steadily increasing influence on the discourse of architecture. He traces the historical emergence of the architectural diagram to the late eighteenth century, citing Jean-Nicholas-Louis Durand for his claims that early diagrams considered themselves a means of developing a universal language: "drawing serves to render account of ideas … it serves to fix ideas, in such a way that one can examine anew at one's leisure, correct them if necessary, it serves finally to communicate them afterwards, whether to clients or different contractors."[78]

The special resonance of the photograph is understood to come from a privileged connection to reality. As Barthes famously stated, "certainly the image is not the reality, but at least it is its perfect analogon."[79] The diagram, on the other hand, is privileged as a figure of use and transformation—not a representation of reality but something more akin to a stand-in. The diagram—as a mode of representational practice—marks a shift from a concern with the perceptual qualities of the object to a concern with its undergirding conceptual relationships. No longer mimesis—but rather system. This form of drawing transforms the concepts of the image and the object, the real and the virtual—as well as understandings of vision and visuality. It articulates a different approach to aesthetics—this process of making sense.

Whereas incipient virtual reality systems would tumble headlong into traditional representational models in their zeal to create a believable visual world around the user, the films of Zajac and Siden do not propose to trick us into believing that what we are seeing is anything immediately familiar to our lived, phenomenological experience. Composed of abstractions and filled with symbols, they were marked by steadily shifting perspectives and top-down or cross-sectioned views that were unbeholden to the physics of a mechanical camera in the physical world. As such, Sinden and Zajac saw them as affording the unique ability to visualize concepts *that had never before been amenable to photographic representation*. Although employing the material substrate of celluloid film, neither offered "a deposit of the physical object" as might be produced through a process of photographic representation descended from the camera obscura. Instead, they provided an image of a *structural organization* that itself was inimical to photographic capture. This scientific empiricism does not depend on the regime of the photographic for its claim to truth value—and it helped to extinguish the photograph's claim to truth even before digital manipulation ultimately sealed its fate.

Both films are attempts to represent a system by focusing on limited objects that then make up a functional whole. It was a model that represented structure rather than appearance. The "real" of the world is understood through modeling rather than mimesis. This film shows the relations of parts. In this, the satellite is understood not as its appearance but as system. To see something thus is to understand an object as it functions rather than as it appears.[80] To claim this, following Vidler, is to see these drawings as "proposing a world other than that which exists" in a constitutive manner—in other worlds, with real consequences for our understanding of what the world is and how it works. The drawings develop from the model of vision proposed by cybernetics—a diagrammatics of vision that prioritizes abstraction, function, and system above all else. Its potential and its danger lie in the way that it simplifies objects to produce action—an easy, transparent translation between man and machine.

Computer-Generated Pictures was the unassuming title for a groundbreaking exhibition held at the Howard Wise Gallery in New York in 1965. It was the first exhibition of digital art in the United States. But the work it showcased was by scientists working at Bell Labs who didn't necessarily consider themselves artists— Béla Julesz, an experimental psychologist interrogating questions of visual perception, and A. Michael Noll, an engineer working on speech data. Both had become interested in the computer as a tool for visualization and a machine that could shape aesthetics—the ways that things are perceived and known. Both created images as a consequence of practical, applied experiments. Noll used the computer and the microfilm plotter to generate randomly orchestrated linear graphics. Julesz used the computer and the microfilm plotter to answer questions about stereoscopic vision that had been unanswered since they were posed in the 1850s.

But dislocating these works from the lab to the gallery dramatically reframed their reference and function. As experiments in perception and computer graphics were situated alongside contemporary abstract geometric painting and post-Cagean aleatory art, a fascinating cross-cultural dialogue was inaugurated—a premonition of the intersection between the two cultures to which Bell Labs famously became host. And from the beginning, Bell's management was never entirely sure whether to promote or disavow these strange experiments that did not quite fit into the usual categories of either science or development. It is precisely for their curious disjunction—their orthogonal relation to the discourses and practices of their time—that these works command renewed attention.

The works themselves mixed the stark and the playful, the utilitarian and the aesthetic. Some were simulations of paintings framed as an investigation into the creative possibilities of the computer. Many of them were made to be viewed as three-dimensional using polarized glasses, an astonishing conjunction of new and old that paired the latest advances in postwar computational technology with an optical toy invented before the photographic negative one hundred twenty years earlier. These images were essentially impossible to produce prior to the advent of computation and, more specifically, prior to the introduction of the S-C 4020 microfilm plotter as a graphic output technology

In exploring the curious early works of Julesz and Noll, this chapter attends to the context of these works' exhibition and to the aesthetic and technological discourses within which they were positioned. But it also examines the technical and material processes by which these images were made. By so doing, these images can be seen to index the peculiar hybridization in play within these early graphic-computational systems. Shaped by the characteristic affordances of the IBM 7094 and the S-C 4020, these images provide a unique window into the initial development of computational aesthetics.

Computer-Generated Pictures

Noll and Julesz made their images at Bell Lab's New Jersey campus in a space that was dedicated to scientific research and technological innovation. The *Computer-Generated Pictures* exhibition, which ran from April 6 to 24, 1965, took them to midtown Manhattan's Howard Wise Gallery, an eponymous space run by a retired executive from Cleveland. It had started as a "proper 57th Street gallery," opening in 1960 with a show of abstract expressionist paintings typical for the period.[1] But beginning with an exhibition of kinetic art in 1961, Wise became a somewhat improbable evangelist for a technologically savvy strain of avant-garde art that included kinetic sculpture, light art, video art, and computer graphics—anything and everything that used advanced technology in either its fabrication or its exhibition. Wise's gallery rapidly established itself at the crest of a rising wave of interest in the intersection of art and technology.

The gallerist Leo Castelli once described how, in the midst of the many ordinary spaces exhibiting the expected fare, "there are just five or six galleries that at one moment or another play a more important role, come up with new ideas."[2] Against all odds, Wise's gallery turned out to be one of those few places, and his groundbreaking exhibition *Computer-Generated Pictures* one of those rare "new ideas."

Wise exhibited artists who possessed knowledge of science and engineering, but more radically, he also exhibited working scientists and engineers. He approached Béla Julesz in 1964 with an invitation to exhibit his stereograms. Julesz was game so long as disclaimers were attached to the images attesting to their status as scientific experiments rather than works of art. Julesz also suggested that A. Michael Noll, a colleague of his at Bell Labs who then was working with computer graphics, be invited to participate as well. Wise was known for witty, unusual gallery announcements, and this one was no exception. The exhibition showcasing "computer-generated pictures" that were "conceived by Béla Julesz and Michael Noll" and "executed by digital computers" was announced with a set of rectangular tan, green, yellow, and blue IBM punchcards laced with the ordered holes that programmers used to communicate with the computer.[3]

The works in the show carried titles such as *Vertical-Horizontal Number Three*, *Computer Composition with Lines*, and *Ninety Parallel Sinusoids*. All of

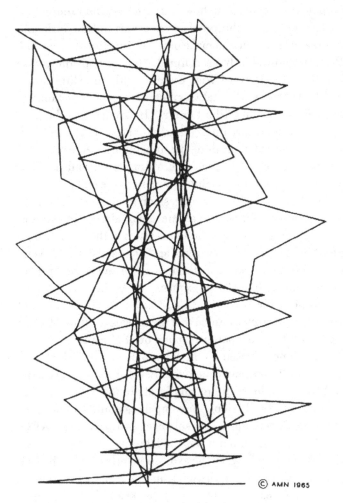

A. Michael Noll, *Gaussian Quadratic* (1965).

the images were photographic enlargements of the S-C 4020's native lines and dots. For some, special polarized spectacles were handed out to allow side-mounted two-dimensional images to appear in curious three-dimensionality. Most of the images are in black and white—simultaneously vibrant and endlessly repetitive. Their straight lines and geometric dynamism speak to the automation that comes with computation and look back to an earlier era of mechanical machines. Noll's *Gaussian Quadratic*, for example, appears as a blitz of black lines scattered over a stark white page. The lines connect into triangles and quadrangles. They run thickest around the middle of the page and become more diffuse and scattered toward the edges. The overall effect is one of movement—an oscillation around a central pole that seems somehow both ordered and random.

This was the first public exhibition of computer art in New York, and art critics did not really know what to make of it.[4] Writing for the *New York Times*, Stuart Preston ambivalently proclaimed, "the wave of the future crashes significantly at the Howard Wise Gallery" with an exhibition of images "executed by IBM 7094 Digital Computer with the assistance of General Dynamics SC-4020 Microfilm Plotter."[5] He argued that the process of making the works was more interesting than the specific results on display, claiming that the collaboration—presumably between man and machine but also between the S-C 4020 microfilm plotter and the IBM 7094 computer—was "revolutionary."[6] But he lamented the end product as "bleak geometry" without even a minor concession to manual sensibility. Worse, for Preston, it looked forward to a time when "almost any kind of painting can be computer-generated—the actual touch of the artist will no longer play any part in the making of a work of art."[7] The artist would eventually be reduced to the producer of mathematical formulas, he opined, and the works would emerge like a "deus ex machina."[8] Other writers concurred with the sentiment: the *New York Herald Tribune* called the work "cold and soulless," and *Time* magazine claimed that the images exhibited had all the aesthetic appeal "of the notch patterns found on IBM cards."[9]

Even Bell Labs was nonplussed by the Wise Gallery exhibition. Noll claims that research staff and management at Bell Labs were very supportive but that AT&T's public relations and legal groups were less sanguine. They worried that the Bell Telephone companies would look askance at any attempts to frame "computer art" as sober scientific research. AT&T attempted to halt the exhibition, but it was too late. Instead, AT&T asked Julesz and Noll to restrict publicity for the exhibition, attesting to the lack of value that the company placed on the work and its fear that the public might react poorly to the idea of art as research. Julesz and Noll were even asked to take out copyrights in their own names to create a further distance—a process that proved to be more complicated than they might have assumed. Noll tried to register *Gaussian Quadratic* with the US Copyright Office at the Library of Congress, another body perplexed by the works on display. His request was originally denied "since a machine had generated the work."[10] He explained that a human being had written the program that, through a mix of randomness and order, generated the work. The Library of Congress again declined: randomness was unacceptable. Noll finally argued that although the numbers produced by the program appeared random, "the algorithm generating them was perfectly mathematical and not random at all," and the work was finally patented.[11]

Reviews of the exhibition seemed to acknowledge the significance of the exhibition and even the importance of the S-C 4020 as a crucial, albeit peripheral, component in these works. But reviewers tended to cast their gaze longingly back to a past where the artist was an artisan and where the artist's individual, subjective expression was conveyed directly through the ancient mark-making of the human hand. These critics failed to recognize the manner in which Julesz and Noll's works, despite their novel mode of manufacture, fit perfectly within the minimal, cool aesthetic that was then establishing its ascendancy. Anti-emotive rigor, attention to schema and pattern—these things were not unknown to modern art history. They constituted a significant thread leading from the constructivists and the Bauhaus, through Piet Mondrian and de Stijl, and to the minimal and conceptual models then emerging in the wake of John Cage's postexpressionist aesthetics. But simultaneously, these works were in dialogue with fundamental questions of optics and perception that suffuse the early history of modernism and had recently returned to the fore with Ernst Gombrich's *Art and Illusion*, gestalt psychology, and the postwar recovery of Marcel Duchamp's research into what the artist called "precision optics."

Art Ex Machina

Neither Julesz nor Noll had originally set out to make computer art or even to interrogate computer graphics. When Noll arrived at the research division of Bell Labs, he was working on a project that plotted speech data. The key tool for this was the recently manufactured S-C 4020 microfilm plotter. One day, his officemate came back with a computer-generated data graph that had gone haywire because of a programming error; instead of an orderly representation of data, it showed lines that resembled nothing so much as modern abstract painting. Noll and his officemate joked about "computer-generated" abstract art, and Noll found himself unexpectedly serious about the idea. His superior, John R. Pierce, was then investigating computer music, and Noll decided to investigate computer art, using the IBM 7090 digital computer and the S-C 4020 peripheral. According to Noll, "this hardware became the basis for my investigations of computer art."[12]

Noll had been using the S-C 4020 to visualize data, and he now set himself to the task of creating what he called "patterns." In an internally published technical memorandum from 1962 entitled "Patterns by 7090," he describes the mathematical and programming techniques that could be used with the S-C 4020 to venture into the field of visual arts.[13] In producing his first early works such as *Gaussian Quadratic*, Noll used two subroutine packages for the S-C 4020: one draws a series of straight lines "connecting successive points of some previously specified array," and another "simply plots dots at the points specified."[14] In other words, the vertical end points were specified precisely, but the horizontal points were generated with a certain degree of randomness. The memo details eight of these sorts of patterns, with potential variations. As discussed in chapter 1, one thing that is made possible by using the IBM 7090 in conjunction with the S-C 4020 is the rapid construction of families of related films or images. Beginning with a particular set of parameters in a program, it is easy to tweak particular aspects of the image generation to produce series of works with slight but significant differences.

Noll took these technical constraints and used them to produce "haphazard" patterns that mix randomness and order "in mathematically specified proportions to achieve a desired effect."[15] The black and white print was an experiment in the visual effects of programmed randomness; straight lines combined "elements of order with the disorder of randomness."[16] Noll was interested in restricting the chaotic effects of purely random number distribution with a sort of pseudo-randomness that was calculated to generate a pleasing appearance. A genuinely random number distribution will wind up with peculiar patterns, such as a lengthy stretch that repeats the number 7. The computer instead generates a series of numbers that *appears* to be random, that approaches the properties of random numbers, but manages to retain a somewhat uniform distribution.[17] Noll's works display a tension between randomness and pseudo-randomness and between chance and control, generated with a subroutine he called white noise generator (WNG) that calculated an array of random numbers using a specified standard deviation. The operant tension in the work—between control and disarray and between clearly lineated rationality and disorganization and disintegration— carries through into a number of Noll's other works.

Randomness manifests in postwar art under a variety of headings—chance, uncertainty, accident, contingency, indeterminacy, play. It is invoked for diverse and divergent aims, from sidestepping consciousness, vacating and repossessing agency, to disrupting originality and its discontents, and redefining the nature of authorship. Chance and randomness were broadly adopted as strategies in art of the 1950s and 1960s in ways that often invoked computation, but it was rare for artists to use computers because they were prohibitively expensive and difficult to access. As Noll pointed out in some of his writings, even if one of these costly machines might be available, there was a barrier because of the technical knowledge that was necessary to program the machine.[18]

Noll's randomness was similar, in a number of ways, to that adopted by John Cage and other postwar artists. Cage used the *I Ching* and other forms of cleromancy as the basis for his aesthetic decisions. But he primarily worked with quasi-randomness to delimit his results in a variety of ways while still declaring his interest as "not to bring order out of chaos."[19] He acknowledged the value of pure randomness as a mode but was more interested in "random order" generated through sets of permutational systems. These systems were generally complicated algorithms that countered what he understood as a tendency for artists to regress into both expressionism and preorganized routines. Recapping Cage's argument, his student Allan Kaprow stated that "when one is left to intuition the risk is great that one becomes too dependent on 'inspiration' (an extremely unreliable mistress) and so falls into the trap of coming up constantly with clichés and habits."[20] This drive to escape habit and cliché led artists into considering algorithms and system as a means to conjure a different mode of art that sidestepped of questions of intention.

Noll did not situate *Gaussian Quadratic* within this field of post-Cagean aesthetics. It is unclear precisely how much he knew about Cage's aleatory aesthetic systems or the concrete poetics of someone like Jackson MacLowe. But he did understand the work as recalling the paintings of Pablo Picasso—a quintessential instance of what the art historian Erwin Panofsky terms "pseudomorphosis," defined as "the emergence of a form A, morphologically analogous to, or even identical with, a form B, yet entirely unrelated to it from a genetic point of view."[21] But pseudomorphorsis or not, this unexpected congruence led Noll to consider the possibility of an algorithmic painting. He felt that he had discovered it in the geometric works of Piet Mondrian.

Noll described Mondrian's *Composition with Lines* from 1917 as an assortment of vertical and horizontal bars that, "at first glance, seem to be randomly scattered."[22] But on further study, Noll felt that Mondrian carefully planned the position and placement of each bar following a "scheme or program."[23] Noll carefully set out to analyze Mondrian's works to uncover their "exact algorithm."[24] *Composition with Lines* imagined the surface of the painting as a flat field, regularized by a grid of abstract black and white. It is complete, obsessive, and rigorously ordered, both perfectly clear and essentially opaque. It left itself wide open to the kind of analysis that Noll bought to bear on it. He examined the length of the lines. He considered their distribution. Each bar was a data point to be scrutinized, both in itself and in the ways that it functioned within the total field of relations established within the painting.

As Noll explained, he understood the painting as a field that could be expressed as numerical data that could be then inversely transformed back into a painting. Noll found that the Mondrian was uniquely suitable in that it fit within the structural limitations of the S-C 4020, the graphical output device with which Noll had to work. When he felt that he understood the framework, Noll set out to create a program "to generate a computer Mondrian," which he called *Computer Composition with Lines*.[25] The resulting print looks remarkably Mondrian-like. It is a precisely ordered gridded field of obsessive hatchmarks neatly laid down. Look again, though: Noll has upped the random factor. The algorithm has been tweaked. The computer has been pulled in to create something that speaks to a carefully elaborated *disorder*.

Noll's work interrogating the role of the computer in art aspires to be simultaneously serious and playful. It proposes something that is both analytic and generative. By envisioning the bars as points in a field of data, Noll has opened up an understanding of Mondrian's paintings as a map of relationships—as rubrics that generate images in logical progression. Noll imagined the elements of an individual work as points of data and their arrangement as, quite literally, programming.[26]

Noll's Mondrian experiment led him to look for more recent work that might be considered "algorithmic," and to his surprise, he quickly discovered that looking for mathematically structured paintings in 1965 was like shooting fish in a barrel. Between the excitement of the space race and the fervor over the new media theories of Marshall McLuhan, technology and automation were "in" with a vengeance. Noll turned his eye, as well as his computer and microfilm plotter, toward Bridget Riley, whose paintings were instrumental in cementing the art world's extraordinary (albeit extraordinarily short-lived) fascination with op art. Riley was doubly relevant to Noll: not only was her work rigorously ordered in a way that seemed programmatic, but it also was concerned with the fundamental nature of human perceptual systems. Noll's *Ninety Parallel Sinusoids with Linearly Increasing Period* is thus both formally and structurally aligned with Riley's *Current* of 1964. Noll was fascinated by the exactness of the painting's vibratory motion, which he found could be precisely quantified using sine waves with a linearly increasing period. And yet Noll's recapitulation of Riley's work invites an explicit comparison between the kind of work exhibited at the *Computer-Generated Pictures* show and the Museum of Modern Art's blockbuster exhibition *The Responsive Eye*, which was taking place just a few blocks away.

William Seitz had organized *The Responsive Eye* exhibition around the new "optical" or "retinal" art that had sprung up over the previous few years. The MoMA exhibition was the apex for a body of work that began under the sign of "kineticism" and "virtual movement" in Europe with artists like Victor Vasarely.[27] *The Responsive Eye* showcased geometric

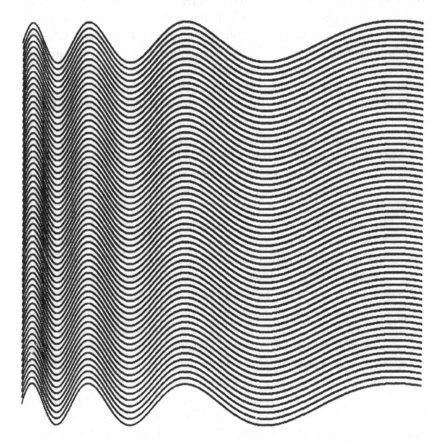

A. Michael Noll, *Ninety Parallel Sinusoids with Linearly Increasing Period* (1965).

abstraction and shimmering pattern, providing a forum for a broad range of artists and even a few scientists to explore questions of vision. Seitz used the term *perceptualism*, but the popular press ran with *op art*, a term generally credited to Jon Borgzinner, the *Time* magazine art critic, who described them as "pictures that attack the eye."[28]

The critical rhetoric that surrounded the show was mixed, to say the least. Seitz framed it as a serious investigation into questions of perception, and his discourse was liberally dusted with scientific terminology. His catalog essay suggests that the paintings in the show weigh in on long-standing issues in perceptual psychology such as "whether the phenomenon of simultaneous contrast of colors was physiological, as Ewald Hering contended, or psychological, as Hermann von Helmholtz claimed" before turning to contemporary scientific investigators who claim that optical illusions put "in question any belief in 'objective' perception."[29] For Seitz, the "responsive eye" was a rational eye, a scientific eye, a cautious, detached eye that looked backward to the revolution in theories of vision that took place in the nineteenth century. Simultaneously, however, Seitz refers to contemporary perceptual psychology, claiming that "it is only recently that a meeting ground is being established on which artists, designers, ophthalmologists and scientists can meet to expand our knowledge and enjoyment of visual perception."[30] Seitz went on to note that "the visual impact of mechanization, modular building, automation and cybernetics everywhere around us has also influenced perceptual art."[31]

Such rhetoric might lead one to imagine a heavily academic exhibition that could provoke only a specialist's interest, but the reality was the opposite. The exhibition proved so popular that it soon found itself roundly attacked as commercial spectacle by the art-critical establishment. Instead of inviting sustained aesthetic contemplation, critics accused these works of attacking the eye, of "preying and playing on the fallibility of vision" to seduce it with the dazzlement of base visual trickery.[32] But the universality of this "trickery"—its immediate engagement and somatic charge—formed the basis of its popular and scientific appeal. Seitz argued that the works in the exhibition were part of a "diversiform international development" that he termed "the new perceptual art.... the terrain on which they operate is not that of the outside world or even the surface of the canvas, but the incompletely explored region between the cornea and the brain."[33] The critics that discussed *Computer-Generated Pictures* did not align it with the show down the street. But the shows were connected by their interest in the psychophysiology of human visual perception, even though they approached it from different angles. Julesz's work, in particular, set out to explore similar territory.

The Cyclopean Eye

The area "between the eye and the brain" was precisely what Julesz was interrogating in his work on display at the *Computer-Generated Pictures* exhibit at the Howard Wise Gallery. Julesz showed a number of random dot patterns that were meant to be viewed with polarized lenses handed out to visitors by the gallery. The terminology applied to a number of the paintings at *The Responsive Eye* exhibit at the Museum of Modern Art is apropos here. Rhythmic and decidedly machinic, Julesz's works are random sets of latticed dots and lines. When viewed through the glasses, they resolve in hovering planes of lacework, with a startling depth that is invisible to the unaided eye. Julesz was interested in how this shift took place and where. He argued that it happened in something he called the "cyclopean eye" of the viewer, as Julesz referred to the visual cortex—the perceptual center in the brain that supersedes the retina.

Although the central point of *The Responsive Eye* exhibit seemed to be its strange effects on the viewer, Julesz looked to find out precisely where those effects were taking place to explore how vision worked on a fundamental level. To do so, he combined the possibilities of the computer and the S-C 4020 with a much older technology—the stereoscope. This situated his work in a long line of devices called optical or philosophical toys that were both scientific research and popular entertainment.

Dr. Béla Julesz was a Hungarian engineer who emigrated to the United States in 1956. His work at Bell Labs initially focused on the compression of image data, but after various techniques failed to accomplish the objective, he realized that he required a better fundamental understanding of the functioning of the human perceptual system.[34] The terminology that he used to describe this functioning—the cyclopean eye—was appropriated from the mid-nineteenth-century German scientist Hermann Ludwig Ferdinand von Helmholtz, and Julesz's explorations returned to the scientific debates of that period, especially the debate between Charles Wheatstone and David Brewster on the question of binocular perception.

The phenomenon of binocular disparity had been noted and discussed well prior to the nineteenth century. In the third century BC, Euclid and Ptolemy had discussed the differences in perception between the left and right eyes and the basic principles of binocular vision. But as Jonathan Crary points out, not until the 1830s did scientists begin to understand binocular perception as an essential component of a seeing body and solve the riddle of binocular perception: "given that an observer perceives with each eye a different image, how are they experienced as single or unitary?"[35]

In the 1820s, Charles Wheatstone and David Brewster were active in a group of London scientists who were investigating what were often called "philosophical toys"—instruments whose fascinating simplicity allowed them to enjoy a unique status as both scientific experiments and parlor amusements.[36] In 1838, Wheatstone described the means by which two images of slightly different perspectives could be shown such that each eye could see only one, thus creating an illusion of spatial depth. He demonstrated this with an optical toy he called a stereoscope. Initially, Wheatstone illustrated binocular combination with a set of two tubes arranged in a simple box, but the difficulty of using this device led him to develop a stereoscope that had two mirrors at right angles and two vertical picture holders. A later version enabled the user to manipulate the angle of incident, thus changing the nature of the resulting image. Oliver Wendell Holmes said of the experience of viewing it that "the shutting out of surrounding objects, and the concentration of the whole attention, which is a consequence of this, produce a dreamlike exaltation ... in which we seem to leave the body behind us and sail away into one strange scene after another, like disembodied spirits."[37]

How, precisely, this three-dimensional presentation was able to achieve its effects was a topic of a great frustration and debate in the middle of the nineteenth century. An acrimonious feud developed over the topic between Charles Wheatstone and David Brewster, who was an inventor, a scientist, and a member of the British Royal Society. Brewster saw Wheatstone demonstrate his stereoscope at the Royal Society and purchased one to use in his own experiments. But in 1849, he developed his own stereoscope using a box and viewing prisms to fuse two side-by-side pictures. In October 1856, Brewster authored a scathing anonymous letter to the *Times* claiming that Wheatstone stole the idea of the stereoscope from James Elliot, a mathematics instructor in Edinburgh who authored plans for such an instrument in 1834. He then criticized both Wheatstone and Elliot for not using the then newly discovered photographic process to view image pairs rather than line drawings.[38] Brewster's arguments of priority were successfully refuted, but they actually circled around his real point—a basic disagreement over the physiological mechanism of binocular vision. Each thought of stereoscopic phenomena in a fundamentally different way. For Wheatstone, each eye itself perceived a distinct image, and these two images later were fused into a singular image by the mind. Helmholtz later articulated this position very clearly, stating that in binocular vision,

> two distinct sensations are transmitted from the two eyes, and reach the consciousness at the same time and without coalescing; that

accordingly the combination of these two sensations into the single picture of the external world of which we are conscious in ordinary vision is not produced by any anatomical mechanism of sensation, but by a mental act.[39]

By contrast, Brewster essentially sought to reassimilate binocular vision to monocular vision. For him, the physiological mechanism of perception was located in the eye itself rather than in the mind. As he stated, "we know nothing more than that the mind, residing as it were, in every point on the retina, refers the impression made upon it at each point to a direction coinciding with the last portion of the ray which conveys the impression."[40] Julesz writes that, in beginning his study of stereoscopic vision, he had been

> startled to learn that according to the prevalent notions of psychologists at the time, stereopsis was an enigmatic problem, based on monocular form-recognition, shrouded in the mystery of semantics, and complicated by the many familiarity cues that are needed to recognize, say, a face ... As a former radar engineer, I knew that this view of psychologists could not be valid. After all, in order to break camouflage in aerial reconnaissance, one could view aerial images (taken from two somewhat different positions) through a stereoscope and the camouflaged target would jump out in vivid depth.[41]

Julesz was familiar with stereo photographs from balloons and airplanes that were not entirely unlike random-dot stereograms. He determined, from looking at these images of camouflage and hiding, that the cues and contours of monocular form were not necessary and essential for stereopsis—a conclusion that went against then-prevalent beliefs. He drew in part on the work of visual theorist James Gibson, who developed his theory of vision during World War II through his research on airplane pilots. Gibson argued that visual space should not be conceived of "as an object or an array of objects in air" as it has been in the past but rather as a "ground theory" exploring "a continuous surface or an array of adjoining surfaces."[42] He developed an interest in texture gradients as they shaped slant and depth perceptions but never advanced to the question of binocular vision as Julesz did.

Essentially, Julesz felt that there were two critical points of debate: where does stereopsis occur, in the eye or in the mind, and is monocular form recognition of contours necessary to generate stereopsis? Before Julesz's experiments, the general understanding of the mechanism of human visual perception was that each eye scrutinized the object and each eye individually recognized that object. Monocular form recognition came first, and only after this process was complete were the two ocular inputs combined into a binocular image. Stereopsis—the visual perception of a three-dimensional world—could occur only after monocular recognition and combination. Julesz showed that this was not only an incomplete understanding of stereopsis but that it was, in a certain sense, incorrect.

Julesz felt that work in perceptual science had foundered on a methodological problem caused by its reliance on the line drawing. Scientists and psychologists studying perception had long used simple line drawings as their primary tool for investigation. These drawings were shown to research participants, and general conclusions were postulated based on these experiments. But for Julesz, line drawings were problematic sources from which to draw valid conclusions about human perception. First, as long as the drawing was not abstract, the human subject would always resort to the habituated recognition of objects in an image, and this subjective, learned response would inevitably disrupt investigation into the objective, physiological mechanisms involved. Second and perhaps more important, line drawings did not offer any continuum of light and dark, color and contrast. As such, they were significantly divorced from the rich and variegated perceptual stimuli of the real world, with its intricate textural range and near-continuous variation.

Using the Computer to Reinvent the Stereoscope

At Bell Labs, Julesz realized that he could break through this impasse by using the digital computer and the microfilm printer to generate random dot patterns of continuous depth and complexity. To the naked eye, these patterns would appear abstract—blurry fields of textured squares. Their surface was a stubborn range of seemingly random smudges lacking any immediately discernible content. Images like these would not have been impossible to create prior to computation, but they would have been prohibitively difficult to produce in sufficient quantities to be useful for scientific investigation. As Julesz stated, "if I had taken a year after I had the idea ... I could have done the demonstration of some of these ideas without the computer."[43] He could have created the twenty thousand points in the image by hand, after manually making the necessary calculations, but for Julesz, "the mere notion of going into something so terribly complicated had prevented it. I found it ridiculous."[44] Yet the computer now made the production of these extraordinarily complex images into a relatively simple matter.

To make his random-dot stereograms, Julesz programmed the computer to create sets of random patterns. These patterns are made up of, essentially, randomly selected black and white mosaic tile—only each tile is a letter on the Charactron screen, specifically selected for its brightness level. The sixty-four type characters of the microfilm printer allowed for a sufficient variation in brightness level and "provided an efficient means for plotting brightness information."[45] The grid size available with the microfilm output was 1024 × 1024—over a million plottable points.

Into this random array, introduce any clear-cut figure—say, a diamond—and draw it into the surface of the array, not with lines or contours and not in a way that is legible to ordinary vision. Instead, frame a diamond in the center of the image. Now take this diamond, with its random array of brightness points, its bright and dark dots, and shift it to the left. This leaves a blank space where the dots have been moved, and that space is then filled up with more random dots. Then the same thing is done on an identical copy of the original image, but the diamond is displaced slightly to the right, which creates another blank space that is then filled with random dots. At this point, you have two images—two halves of a stereogram. Looking at them directly, Julesz compared the appearance of these surfaces to sandpaper; they are richly noisy surfaces. The displaced diamonds are invisible to the eye, subsumed in the general chaos of the surface. But looked at through a stereoscope, the images fuse, and after a moment, the diamond appears—not outlined, not contoured, but strangely sharp and uncannily floating over the background of the image. This hovering diamond solves the debate between Wheatstone and Brewster about the priority of binocular and monocular vision, and it contradicted the commonly held understanding of Julesz's time by stressing the stereopsis can and does occur in the complete absence of monocular form. Julesz also emphasizes that "if monocular form exists, stereopsis precedes perception of this form and can scramble it."[46]

Julesz used random-dot stereograms to "portray information on the "mind's retina"—that is, at a place where the left and right visual pathways combine in the visual cortex."[47] The binocular information is independent of the monocular information. He went on to state,

Where your external eyes were presented with randomness, your cyclopean eye receives something new and definite. A clear-cut diamond is perceived hovering over the random-dotted background. Here there is a sharp, determinate, distinctive perception of form that must originate somewhere in the visual nervous system beyond the retinae of the eyes. As psychologists, then, we have to a certain extent

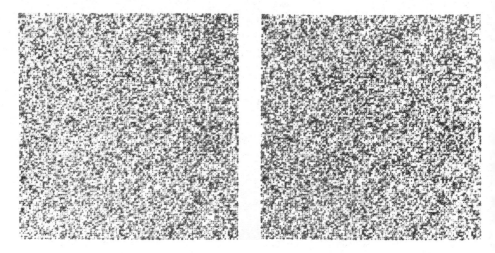

Béla Julesz, *Random-Dot Stereogram*, in *Foundations of Cyclopean Perception* (Cambridge, MA: MIT Press, 2006), reprinted with permission.

managed to look into the "black box" of the visual system: we have found out something about where a particular perceptual process takes place.[48]

In his research, Julesz set out to trace the flow of visual information in the brain, a "psychoanatomical" survey that used sets of images instead of scalpels and used them to greater effect than magnetic resonance imagery (MRI) as far as determining priority. He described himself as looking for the "cyclopean eye," the space where the views of the two eyes combine into a single image replete with depth. Helmholtz had used the term to refer to a hypothetical single eye—"the 'mind's eye,' that 'sees' a single stereoscopic image given appropriate stimuli in the two eyes"[49] Fittingly, the Cyclops is a mythical creature. Julesz claimed that

> the essence of cyclopean stimulation is this formation of a percept at some central location in the visual system by using stimuli that could not possibly produce that percept at an earlier location. It is as though we were operationally "skipping" the peripheral processes and stimulating some central location.[50]

Julesz sought to establish a separation and a priority between the central and the peripheral processes. With his classic text *Foundations of Cyclopean Perception,* he argues that his basic question is one of "the tracing of the information flow in the visual system, particularly the separation of peripheral (retinal) processes from central (cerebral) ones."[51] Julesz's random-dot stereograms conclusively proved that depth perception did not occur in the eye itself but in a complicated optical-neurological process. His random dots allowed him to see that binocular localization is, in fact, prior to monocular vision—and thus prior to the recognition of form, sidestepping "the formidable problems of sematics."[52]

In *Techniques of the Observer*, Jonathan Crary focuses on the historical and epistemological shift from the camera obscura, which he sees as emblematic of a distanced and detached model of vision, to the stereoscopes of Wheatstone and Brewster, in which vision becomes newly corporeal, a phenomenon that is engendered in the body. Despite their argument over the precise location of the visual process, the process remains ineluctably somatic, rooted in the concrete physiological mechanisms of the human body. Julesz was able to demonstrate a process about which Wheatstone and Helmholtz could only speculate. Perception, for Julesz, was revealed as a process that occurs without our conscious volition. Recognition was displaced onto a secondary plane, removing the question of memory that had been important to the study of contour. Julesz was able to demonstrate that without any training and without our input, vision just happens: it constitutes a "rapid, effortless, and spontaneous process."[53] Where Noll's images were investigations into the possibilities of computer graphics, Julesz created his stereograms to probe the architecture of vision.

Perspectival Systems

Following Julesz's work on random-dot stereograms, Noll decided that depth perception could be potentially useful in the presentation of scientific curves, graphs, and figures: "The obvious next step was to use the digital computer to calculate and plot stereographic projections of general-purpose scientific data," a technique that he developed in his research and described in his 1965 paper "Stereographic Projections by Digital Computer."[54] Therein, Noll details his production of two perspective drawings, "corresponding to the images seen by the left and right eye. Usually, the drawing of such perspectives is quite tedious and in practice various approximations such as isometric one vanishing point and two vanishing point projections are used."[55] Like Julesz, he points out that although these calculations would have been relentlessly monotonous for a human engineer, the computer was perfectly suited to such repetitive tasks.

When creating a perspective drawing via computer, the first step is to choose a point from which to view the represented object or scene.

Descriptive geometry labels this a "station point." An imaginary plane—the picture plane—hovers between the object and the station point—the point of view. Thus far, it might as well be the time of Alberti—the production technique is virtually unchanged since the Renaissance. But as Noll continues to explain, two perspectives are necessary to create a stereographic drawing, and two station points have to be selected. And this is firmly in the realm of the computational, with the ease of calculating and changing the viewpoint on a given object, as depicted in the shifting perspectives in Zajac's and Sinden's films.

As J. R. Pierce, Noll's boss, points out: "this is serious work. Scientists and engineers want to present data in graphical and even in moving form, and they want to see what proposed devices and structures will look like from various angles."[56] The computer can make these drawings and animations much more quickly and easily than even a highly trained draftsman. And in Noll's description of his work, his examples of three-dimensional drawings include a contour plot of electrical transfer function, a three-dimensional speech spectrogram, and a block diagram. His other example is of less immediate use but is arguably more interesting—a random pattern of straight lines, a "three-dimensional bundle of lines whose end points have been determined at random."[57] He argues, following Julesz, that this image is useful for demonstrating depth, since, like Julesz's images, "each perspective by itself contains no monocular perspective clues."[58] And again, because any of these images can be viewed from any distance and any angle, an infinity of rotation and alignments is possible.

"If the rectangular coordinates of some point are known, then the corresponding left and right perspectives can be easily computed," and "the introduction of angles of inclination and rotation of the viewing point makes the computations only slightly more complex."[59] The object to be projected is fed to the computer in a schema of points, along with the parameters for projection, and "the computer then computes" producing the appropriate equivalent coordinates for the right and left picture-plane views. The object to be represented is limited to straight lines connecting points. This is a functional constraint of the microfilm plotter, which takes on the remaining problem: "to plot the projected points and to then connect lines between them thereby producing the left and right perspectives. This is a job far too tedious to do by hand; fortunately, an elaborate device manufactured by the Stromberg-Carlson division of General Dynamics is available for plotting digital data."[60]

The process is similar to that used to compute films. Noll inputs the points to be projected into the IBM 7094 digital computer, which runs them through a stereographic projection program. A subroutine called ARRAY "is called to store the coordinates of the points of each set. After all of the sets of points have been called, a call to PLOT computes the stereographic projections, using the previously derived equations."[61] PLOT specifies distance to origin, the interfocus distance, and the resulting angles of inclination and rotation. Again, only the endpoints need be computed; the microfilm plotter draws the lines between them.

Pierce describes Noll's Mondrian experiment, but he also uses the stereoscope images to point out that Noll "has taken the computer far beyond imitation ... even pairs of drawings which, when viewed through a stereoscope, give the effect of many lines hanging in space."[62] Noll's work here is far from the modernist flat picture plane that served as a fundamental reference for Mondrian and, to a certain extent, for Riley. If anything, it is a step back into the hallucinatory depth of early perspectival drawings—with its conflation of perspective and process. However, as Pierce said, these are not imitations of prior work. The relentless technical precision required to produce random three-dimensional stereograms makes them unlike single-point perspective drawings. Stereoscopic images generally required the automatic production of the camera, the imprint of the world generated through optics set slightly apart. Noll's drawings would have been impossibly difficult to calculate or produce prior to the advent of a computer linked to a drafting device. The automatic production and the visual geometry are produced with this conjunction.

Computational Aesthetics

When planning the *Computer-Generated Pictures* exhibit for the Howard Wise Gallery, Noll and Julesz agreed to split the profits and were disappointed that not a single work sold. It was hard to understand, given the collector's frenzy then going on around Riley and many other op artists. The works seemed, in some ways, to inhabit a similar conceptual space and, as Noll was aware, could look very similar. Why, then, were they received differently?

One point is that regardless of their pattern, Riley, like most of the op artists, worked within a tradition of painting. Her works could be held up as "advanced" or "ground-breaking" painting, but although they operated at the edge of the respectable, they were firmly on the inside, safe edge. Op art was interested in the same questions that Julesz and Noll were asking and took on some of the same lineage, but Riley's work made these questions playful and somewhat comforting while maintaining a frisson of the avant-garde.

By contrast, the work of Noll and Julesz anticipated the conceptual work of the next decade by refusing aesthetic material trappings and posing hard questions about the purpose and place of art in an advanced consumer society. The works of Julesz and Noll asked difficult questions about the changing nature of visual production and perception, and they asked them in languages and with materials that were arduous and uncomfortable for the general population. It was easy to go to an op art show, feel a certain dizziness after staring extendedly at a vertiginous black and white painting, and return home. To stare at Julesz and Noll's work at *Computer-Generated Pictures* was to stare at the language of incipient computation, the mechanization of human enterprise and to confront the uncertainties of the coming economic and cultural transformations that were sure to ensue.

Some of this anxiety was clear in the critical reviews of the show. Critics appreciated that something interesting was going on, but their immediate response was to look away. They were afraid that what was interesting was not the work, or even the artists, but rather the machines and their newfound capacities. The reviews are afraid of the coming future, which the critics see as both fascinating and terrifying. There was a market for playful pop and the waning heroic abstract expressionism of the previous decade, but for these computer-drawn works, there was no market.

There was an audience, however. Rather than looking to the past of the handcrafted, as the initial reviews of the *Computer-Generated Pictures* exhibit seemed to do, Julesz and Noll looked to a future of conceptualism and process-based work that moved past the realm of the object. They were working to reinvent the possibilities of media in a way that continued to resonate in the 1960s and 1970s with algorithmic and process-based work but even more clearly into a future of software art and generative graphics.

Beginning in 1966, Kenneth Knowlton and Leon Harmon made a series of images called Studies in Perception. *The first of these became an iconic work of early computer art, widely reproduced but rarely discussed. These images, individually and as a series, interrogate the possibilities of the S-C 4020 and the Charactron tube by staging a dialogue between photography and computation at a moment when the two were not intuitively linked except in apparatuses like the S-C 4020. The images imagine perception as something that swerves between visibility and invisibility, legibility and illegibility, and human and machine.*

Rather than taking place in the realm of science, like the works of Béla Julesz and A. Michael Noll, their interrogation of perception was staged in the literal and figurative idiom of pop art, thus inserting computer visualization as a central term within a broader conversation about representation in late modern aesthetics. The Studies in Perception *series is an artifact of a particular moment in the late 1960s when there was an uneasy rapprochement between art and technology within a rapidly changing discourse of aesthetics. Simultaneously, in the realm of computer graphics, it pointed toward an understanding of computer visualization as something undergirded not by vectors but by grids.*

From Lab to Museum

Studies in Perception I began as a practical joke. Kenneth Knowlton and Leon Harmon, two engineers at Bell Labs, planned to surprise vacationing executive Ed David with a twelve-foot long "modern art" mural—a pop art confection of surface pattern and symbol, "a huge picture made of small electronic symbols for transistors, resistors and such" that would surprise the retreating viewer in a striptease of sorts.[1] The problem was that after the mural was hung in the executive's office, the intricately tangled bits and pieces that went into a circuit diagram were no longer visible. From the outside corridor or the doorway to the office, the image was a reclining female nude. It was a punch line without a joke, and the upper administration of Bell Labs was less than amused. A détente: Knowlton and Harmon were allowed to use the image as long as they kept the name Bell Labs out of it and did not display it in the office. So after a single day, *Studies in Perception I*, code-named *Nude*, was relegated to a basement rec-room.[2]

But *Nude* was not destined to stay in the basement of the Lab. It resurfaced in a radically different institutional context—the world of avant-garde art. In October 1967, a large-scale print of Knowlton and Harmon's *Nude* appeared at a press conference media spectacle hosted by painter Robert Rauschenberg at a noisy loft in lower Manhattan. The space was "enlivened by revolving painted discs, film projects, floating pillows and miniskirted girls in paper smocks."[3] The event announced the formation of a new organization called Experiments in Art and Technology (E.A.T.) that would be headed by Rauschenberg and another Bell Labs engineer, Billy Klüver. It intended to forge a "working alliance" between art and technology and between artists and engineers. Politicians, including Senator Jacob J. Javits, showed up to endorse the endeavor, which was to be funded by companies like AT&T and IBM. On October 11, 1967, the *New York Times* printed *Nude* as an above-the-fold illustration in the second section for a story on art and science. It described the image as a "large drawing of a nude generated by a computer" that was "masterminded by two engineers."[4]

Although Bell Labs had previously seen Knowlton and Harmon's work as a somewhat juvenile use of sophisticated image-processing technology, this new context offered cachet. The upper administrators changed their minds about attribution. After the publication of the *Times* article, Bell Labs was eager for Knowlton and Harmon's work to be shown and reproduced, as long as they gave suitable credit to Bell Labs. And appear it would: in 1968, *Studies in Perception* was shown at the Howard Wise Gallery in New York City; in Jasia Reichardt's *Cybernetic Serendipity* exhibition at the Institute of Contemporary Arts (ICA) in London; in *The Machine as Seen at the End of the Mechanical Age*, an exhibition at the Museum of Modern Art (MOMA) in New York that was curated by Karl G. Pontus Hultén, director of the Moderna Museet in Stockholm; and in *Some More Beginnings: Experiments in Art and Technology (E.A.T.)*, an offshoot exhibit of the *Machine* show that took place at the Brooklyn Museum.[5]

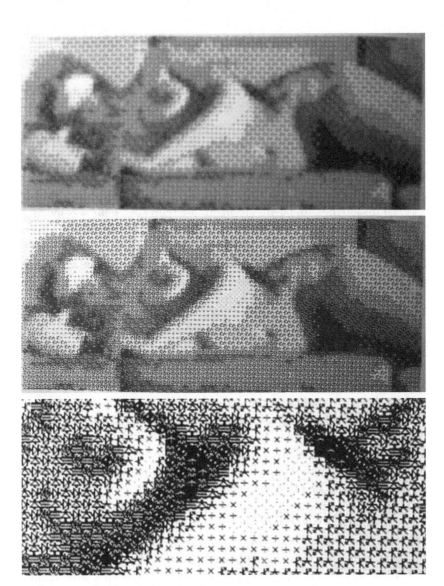

Top: Leon D. Harmon and Kenneth C. Knowlton, *Nude* or *Studies in Perception I* at low resolution, simulating viewing from a distance.
Middle: Leon D. Harmon and Kenneth C. Knowlton, *Nude* or *Studies in Perception I.*
Bottom: Leon D. Harmon and Kenneth C. Knowlton, *Nude* or *Studies in Perception I* viewed close up.

Studies in Perception is at the crux of a complex and multifaceted terrain. It offers a new window on the question of how and why technology came to be a subject of interest to a certain segment of the postwar avant-garde. In this trajectory, an image originally intended as a private joke among engineers was taken up by an art world that was becoming intrigued by a potential alliance between art and technology that would be capable of changing the terrain of aesthetics by interrogating new modes of perception and production. At the moment that *Nude* was being exhibited, art was increasingly understood as a means of investigation and research. For a generation of artists who were coming of age in the 1960s, modernism was fast dissolving into postmodernism, medium specificity was moving into mixed media, and traditional arts such as painting and sculpture were giving way to a dizzying array of practices based on technologies of recording and representation. Photography and film were becoming solidly ensconced within the white walls of the museum. But in contemporary culture, these technologies were being eclipsed by new types of machines and by modes of thinking called "cybernetics," "systems theory," and "information theory." The museum, as an institution, was unsure what to make of these machines and the discourses that they generated.

Studies in Perception is also part of the history of the theoretical and practical innovations that Bell Labs fostered throughout the twentieth century. It is concerned with the space carved out for graphics research at institutions that were not primarily concerned with visual representation, particularly the relationship between computer graphics and photography as differing but potentially intertwined modes of visual representation. Early experiments with computers and photography fell into three categories that were dictated by output constraints. The first category involved raster television screens: computers were used to analyze compression algorithms for television sets, experimenting with how data could most effectively be transmitted.[6] The second involved vector screens, which drove research into considering photographs as a collection of lines. Larry Roberts at MIT scanned photographs of solid objects with simple geometries. The computer then processed this image by detecting the feature points and edges to produce something that resembled a perspectival line drawing of a simple three-dimensional object. This edging is a mode of bandwidth reduction. It makes it possible to display the photographic image on the screen of the computer. Roberts states that "the goal here was to have the machine recognize and understand photographs of three-dimensional objects."[7] The third category, which was by far the most widespread, used microform printers to output photographs after processing. Knowlton and Harmon's experiments fall, to a certain degree, into this category, but they display a tension between the vector screens that were generally used to produce scientific diagrams and the emergent space of the gridded screen, conceptualized here as mosaics. This conceptualization led to an understanding of the screen as composed of *picture elements* or *pixels*.

Making a Computer-Processed Picture

Although other machines were needed to make *Nude*, it is essentially a reflexive engagement with the S-C 4020 that makes both its mechanisms and constraints clear and visible. The surface of the image literally pictures the alphanumeric characters of the Charactron screen. Those characters remain visible and do not defocus into squares. Again, the S-C 4020 remains somewhere in the interstices between the vector screen and the bitmapped pixel screen. Unlike the majority of prior work with the S-C 4020, *Nude* begins with a photograph. The output is also a photograph but

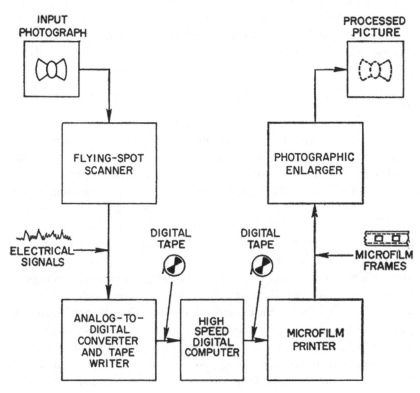

Schematic of a widely used system for computer picture processing. *Source:* Leon D. Harmon and Kenneth C. Knowlton, "Picture Processing by Computer." *Science* 164, no. 3875 (1969): 19–29. [page 19]

one that indexes the characters of the Charactron screen at the heart of the S-C 4020. The output is also not called a *photograph* but *microfilm*, which is conceptualized primarily as an industrial information-storage technology. In short, the daisy-chained machines that made this image are engaged in a complete reimagination of what photography might be in the era of the computer.

Behind *Nude* or *Studies in Perception I* was not just the technical wizardry of Bell Labs but their millions of dollars' worth of equipment. Knowlton and Harmon began with a photographic transparency and used a television-camera-like scanner, an analog-to-digital convertor, magnetic tape, an IBM 7090 programmed with punchcards, the S-C 4020, and a photographic enlarger. But the central platform for *Nude* was the S-C 4020 microfilm plotter.

Knowlton and Harmon did not call their image art or photography, nor did they follow the *New York Times*'s lead and call it a "drawing"; they called it a "computer-processed picture," emphasizing the processing of the image through the computer. From the perspective of contemporary computer systems and their plug-and-play operationality, it is difficult to understand the hybridity of 1960s mainframes, which relied heavily on peripherals. This equipment demanded complicated and nonintuitive transitions between analog and digital and between highly specialized machines. Looking at how *Nude* came into being reveals the complex material conditions that underscored the process of computation at this time and the research field of computer graphics, which was then in its infancy. It also suggests that perhaps it is necessary to attend to present conditions of hybridity—to uneasy translations and transpositions.

Knowlton and Harmon began with a negative—of a photograph of dancer Deborah Hay—that they scanned with a flying spot scanner. The flying spot scanner was used primarily to convert films and other transparencies for television broadcast. It used a television raster screen (a cathode ray tube) to produce a beam of constant luminescence and unmodulated intensity on its surface. The light from this spot was projected with an objective lens onto the surface of the photographic film transparency. The beam traces across the image in a standard scanning pattern, and modulated light emerges on the other side. This goes through a condensing lens and is then converted into a proportional signal by photomultiplier tubes. The flying spot scanner—which Knowlton and Harmon described as "something not entirely unlike a television camera"— thus produced results as analog signals.[8] These were fed into an analog-to-digital converter and tape writer, which output a digitized form of the image on magnetic tape for computer processing.[9]

The magnetic tape went into the computer, whose job was to produce a second magnetic tape to drive the S-C 4020. The computer was an IBM 7094, an update of the previous 7090 mainframe that required a certain stacking of peripherals. Run time on the 7094 was expensive, and it worked faster with magnetic tape than with the punchcards that were the general medium for programming. Cards were fed into a machine that converted their instructions to magnetic tape. Often engineers wrote out card instructions on sheets of paper and gave them to a keypunch operator to produce the punchcards. Both the image and the program (written on punchcards) went through separate machines that eventually were marketed as standalone computers for people who needed less computing power than Bell Labs. The program was written in a version of Fortran (Formula Translation), an imperative programming language created by IBM in the 1950s for scientific and engineering applications and an early high-level computer programming language.

The first sets of codes used to program computers were known as "machine language," which is a sequence of 0s and 1s that the computer understands as electronic instructions. Essentially, machine language is as close as the computer gets to a native language. The second generation of code was "assembly language," a low-level language that has a one-to-one correspondence between written instruction and machine instruction. An assembler converted the written instructions into machine language. Assembly language was specific to a given machine.

After assembly language came higher-level languages and compilers that translated the engineers' written instructions into machine or assembly code. Fortran was an early high-level language that was written for IBM mainframes, was portable between machines, and was more readily legible to the human programmers because it used recognizable words and syntax. Fortran was designed to be easy for engineers to use, and its syntax looked much like ordinary algebraic equations. Fortran made it easier for its primary audience of scientists and engineers to crunch numbers and analyze equations. But it had a limited number of commands, none of which were dedicated to graphic output. Fortran was designed for IBM mainframes whose primary output module was a line printer not unlike a typewriter. Its output was intended to be numbers and to a lesser degree language.

According to Paul Ceruzzi, the acceptance of higher-level languages "illustrates how readily users embraced a system that hid the details of the machine's inner working, leaving them free to concentrate on solving their own, not the machine's, problems."[10] That may be the case, but it certainly did not allow for the complex negotiation of the link between computers and peripherals and the intimate knowledge of their capabilities that was the base for much of computer graphics work at this time. That is where Fortran Assembly Program (FAP) came in. It was a macro Fortran assembler for the IMB 709, 7090, and 7094 computers that allowed the programmer to define and then use macros, further customizing what was possible to do with a given computer system for a given laboratory setup. Ken Knowlton proposed to his superiors that he build a language for making computer animated movies. Essentially, they said, "That sounds difficult, but see what you can do." The Lab did not see an immediate use for the work but found the research promising. His project fell under the auspices of research and development into computer graphics.

In 1963, Knowlton created the BEFLIX (Bell Flicks) computer animation language for the IBM 7090 and the S-C 4020. The hardware drove the conceptualization of the language. One of the central issues in writing the language was that the microfilm recorder understood an extremely limited set of six-bit codes—eighteen in all. Knowlton's BEFLIX allowed these to be combined in various ways to produce films as well as complex images. The microfilm recorder understood the instruction to advance film to the next frame, to select a different camera, and to reset. It understood commands to expand or reduce the image on the screen. It understood display commands—to display a character or a spot at a specified point on the screen at a specified level of brightness. It understood a command to draw a straight-line segment. The commands that produced light on the screen were PLOT, EXPOSE LIGHT, EXPOSE HEAVY, TYPE SPECIFIED POINT, TYPE CURRENT POINT, DRAW VECTOR, GENERATE X-AXIS*, GENERATE Y-AXIS*, and PROJECT FORM. Despite the simplicity of these commands for elementary operations, the machine was able to construct and produce complicated pictures and films from precisely placed lines, points, and characters.

BEFLIX was written as subroutines in MACRO FAP, and Knowlton understood it as having two parts—a "scanner language" and a "movie language." Both of these "are actually macro-instructions. As such, they may be interspersed with instruction of the basic FAP language or, more important, with higher-order macro-instructions which the original programmer has defined in terms of the original movie instructions."[11] The "movie language" involved instructions that control the output or temporary storage of pictures, that perform drafting and typing operations, and that modify rectangular areas. The "scanner language" was the older, primary part of the language, and it was based on imagining that "pictures exist within the 7090 on rectangular surfaces ruled off in squares" with "each square containing a number from 0 to 7. Pictures are created and manipulated by changing the patterns of numbers in the squares. During output these patterns of numbers are interpreted as spots of appropriate shades of grey, according to a programmer-specified transliteration."[12] The storage area within the 7090 was limited—two complete fine-resolution frames, essentially two areas 252 squares wide and 184 squares high.

As stated previously, the heart of the S-C 4020 was the Charactron shaped-beam tube, which was able to generate particular characters at high speed due to a stencil-like matrix. The matrix, a small metal disk, has sixty-four character-shaped holes in a space smaller than a quarter of a square inch: "The electron gun points an electron beam to the matrix through two sets of electrostatic character-selection plates" that deflect the beam so that it goes through a particular aperture, thus shaping it as a particular character. The shaped beam is brightened as it proceeds toward the tube face and deflected to the appropriate position: "From this description, it can be seen that it takes no longer to print an entire CHARACTRON (beam-shaped) character than it does a single dot."[13]

This is a screen that can produce characters as rapidly as points—no mean feat, that. It is rapidly plottable screen that is comprised of 1024 horizontal points by 1024 vertical points—over a million addressable points. But to use the character-printing facility of the Charactron screen—which made it different from all the other vector-point screens on the market—it was necessary to imagine the screen as a grid not of points but of squares. Each character in the matrix occupies a particular amount of space. The characters of the matrix each occupy six horizontal by nine vertical points on the plottable area of the tube face: "These CHARACTRON characters cannot be rotated nor changed in size in any way."[14] Other characters can be created from lines or dots. This means that if the unique abilities of the Charactron (its character-generating facility) are to be used, the screen has to be conceptualized not as an array of points but instead as a grid—an array of separate blocks.

The program for creating *Nude* consisted of several parts: "definitions of new macro instructions, coding for composing the picture, coding for outputting the picture, closed subroutines, and descriptions of text to be typed."[15] The original picture was fragmented into rows. Approximately five thousand points were read as "brightness levels." Instead of creating this level by randomly sprinkling black dots, small square patterns were created that would use the alpha and blank characters of the S-C 4020 to replicate a level of greyscale. For *Nude*, there were eight possible brightness levels; each level had two possible pictures. After the brightness level was determined, the computer randomly selected one of two patterns.

From this, the computer created another digital magnetic tape that was designed for the S-C 4020. The tape went into the microfilm plotter. The Charactron screen glowed in its tiny cubicle while the camera ran in sync, exposing 35 mm microfilm to "print" a part of the picture as a photo negative.[16] The film was developed, and the six sections were sutured together. The six microfilm frames were photographically enlarged, sutured together, and rephotographed. A high-contrast 8- × 10-inch photograph was produced from which large-scale prints could be made. *Nude* was printed at up to 5 × 12 feet—much larger than life size. The image is made up of electronic symbols that are composed of 11- × 11-pixel arrays of the characters alpha and blank. The look, arrangement, and conceptualization of the image and the conceptualization of the BEFLIX program were based on the affordances of the Charactron.

The operating power of the 7090 went to produce a program that could run the microfilm recorder. Parts of the program—the deliberately inserted randomness, particularly—are weighted toward the abilities of the computer. But the conceptualization of the image as a grid and the rendition in characters (rather than more linear halftone shading) led to the specific look of the final print, and they are direct artifacts of the abilities of the S-C 4020. BEFLIX conceptualized the image not as the raster lines of a television screen but as a mosaic. Knowlton called this not an invention of the pixel but an independent discovery of it. More significantly, the S-C 4020 and the BEFLIX language created for it allowed Knowlton and others to understand the computer not as a calculating machine but as a graphical, multimedia machine.

Studies in Perception

This basic procedure was used to produce not only *Studies in Perception I* but also similar works in 1967 and 1968, such as *Telephone, Gulls,* and *Gargoyle* as well as an image of a man interacting with a graphic console using a lightgun. Knowlton and Harmon conceptualized them as part of a series called *Studies in Perception.* In transitioning between multiple registers—photograph, television-camera-like scanner, magnetic tape, computer processing, microfilm print, photograph—these works emphasize the hybrid material conditions that formed the process of computation.

Nude, or *Studies in Perception I,* was the first of the images and was restricted to the alphanumeric characters that were possible through the Charactron screen. Later images used the sized "dots" of the alphanumeric screen to create micropatterns. As Knowlton said, these micropatterns sometimes produced "provocative juxtapositions, such as guns pointing at each other, or bombs falling into cribs," but Bell Labs primary interest was electronics, and so those were the symbols they gravitated toward.[17]

Knowlton and Harmon's terminology—a "computer-processed picture" —emphasizes the layered differential specificity at the heart of this work. But this is not a particular self-explanatory title, and although an understanding of how these works were made is necessary, it does not fully explicate them. To understand this work, it might be necessary to take the title seriously (more seriously than it probably was originally intended)— *Studies in Perception*. The viewer of these "studies in perception" immediately confronts the perceptual trick mentioned earlier. From a distance of a little less than twelve feet, the image shown in *Nude* easily resolves into a reclining nude, a classic subject for art. Yet the subject of the photograph happens to be Deborah Hay, a member of the avant-garde Judson Dance Theater, who had worked with John Cage and Robert Rauschenberg. At that point, she was collaborating with Klüver on the production of a performance work that was itself grounded in tricks of visual perception. As a performer, Hay was concerned with bodies and visuality. Her own artistic practice thus complicates a reading of this image as one that simply belongs to the classical tradition and instead situates it almost as a performance of a body falling into informatic parts at the onset of the computational era.

Move in a little closer, then. The woman steadily becomes less rather than more clearly pictured. The nude fragments into small, squiggly lines, patterns of white on black and black on white. The tonal variation of the image is provided by pattern. At a middle distance, the work is reframed as an experiment in pattern recognition and the limits of abstraction. Move in closer still, and the specificity of the symbols is apparent even as it is impossible to see the image as a whole. Multiplication signs, division signs, electrical symbols: this is the stuff of equations and circuit diagrams. Another possibility presents itself—that this is a work about information and encoding. But the title seems to indicate a larger field of concern—the transformation of representation and even perception itself within an emergent world of computation.

This image, and Knowlton's story of it, appropriates a language of transistors and resistors that is diagrammatic in nature, and does so in the service of figural representation. The diagrams of this picture emerge at the crux of something figured as a problem of perception. Communication is sloppy, and translation is inexact. Noise is dominant rather than subsidiary. Knowlton and Harmon assumed that the symbols would remain meaningful and that the nude would become a kind of jibberish—a secret joke, a quotation underscoring a field of symbols. Instead, the opposite occurred: the symbols became detached from the syntactical structure that would give them meaning. This image incorporates two distinct representational languages—the diagrammatic and the photographic. The image pushes the viewer to see one or the other; it is difficult or even impossible to resolve the symbols and the figural representation simultaneously.

But just as the photograph declines into noise, the symbols, taken as a whole, fail to form a pattern. Disruption is key on every level. The transistor and resistor symbols—described by Knowlton as the essential elements of the pictograph—are taken out of context and kept from becoming part of a meaningful circuit diagram.[18] It is not that most viewers in any venue outside of Bell Labs would have been able to read a circuit diagram, regardless, but rather that this dismemberment resonates.

Noise and pattern had long been key problems for Bell Labs, which were, first and foremost, in the business of signals. In pioneering work on telegraph systems at Bell Labs, Harry Nyquist and Ralph Hartley had shown that text, speech, and images could be considered as equivalents for the purposes of wire transmission. The question then became how to increase the carrying capacity of the lines to be able to transmit more data. Nyquist was one of the engineers who were engaged in the problem of "how to represent the world with electrical signals."[19] Nyquist and Hartley's work developed the telephone line as a transmitter for signal, understood generally—not just voice or telegraph pulses. The signals were considered as "generalized representations of the world."[20] As David Mindell points out, these signals began to resemble digital representation because Nyquist and Hartley used only two symbols, represented by 0 and 1— converting the continuous, analog world into the discrete pulses of binary representation.

Claude Shannon, one of the great minds of Bell Labs, drew on their work to develop information theory. By the time that Knowlton and Harmon were working on computer graphics, Shannon had moved to Boston to teach at MIT. He never officially left the Labs, however, and the Labs never closed his office; it simply grew ever more dusty as the secretary informed callers that he was "out for the day." Information theory, Shannon's legacy, also remained as a crucial part of the ongoing work of Bell Labs in communication. Drawing on Nyquist and Hartley, Shannon's information theory "defines information as a probability function with no dimensions, no materiality, and no necessary connection with meaning. It is a pattern, not a presence.... The theory makes a strong distinction between message and signal."[21] Communication is thus defined as the transferal of this signal through a noisy channel of limited bandwidth.

This language—of signals, noise, and information—became a means of describing the world.

Shannon's work, however, was criticized for decontextualizing information, which was precisely what Nyquist and Hartley were struggling to do. David MacKay, another researcher who was working only a few years later, found himself attempting to formulate "an information theory that would take meaning into account"—where Shannon defined *information* in terms of what it was and MacKay defined it in terms of what it did.[22] To do this is to bring back the recipient as a crucial element of information.

Viewed in duration, *Nude* is an uncomfortable visual pun: it is an image that is legible, if blurred, at a distance and that dissolves on approach into further illegibility. The other *Studies in Perception* at least offer cats and umbrellas as a reward for closeness. *Nude* offers jibberish. The dissolution of "message"—a signal—to noise was precisely what Shannon's information theory was to help prevent. *Nude* asks us to consider "information processing" phenomenologically, implicitly exchanging Claude Shannon's information theory for MacKay's. It inserts the observer back into the loop. In being, in part, about legibility and recognition, it is also about the kind of meaning that emerges in relationships. In a double focus on gestalt perception and then decipherment, there is an insistence on the importance of the information being embodied—being shaped by the particular mechanisms through which it is deployed. These works offer a complex play with the nature of computation. It gives rise to an understanding of an implacable materiality that is tightly bound to, shaped by, and reshaping the human subject.

Art at the End of the Mechanical Age

Knowlton and Harmon's repeatedly shown and reproduced *Studies in Perception I* used the visual language of pop art to consider a relationship that was increasingly complicated and problematic—that of machine age technology and computational technology. Here, the idiom of pop art sutures over a relationship that, in the context of this work, cannot be viewed straight on but only in a flickering, uncertain vision—the shift between models of seeing. In this encounter, the photograph comes to function as a stand-in for an older era of machines and mechanical technology that is associated with the gear and wheel, the car and factory. The diagram becomes emblematic of an encroaching regime of electronic technology that is implemented by the electronic, digital computer. In the late 1960s, the art world was trying to come to terms with this shift from the mechanical to the electronic age.

Studies in Perception was exhibited at two shows that marked the late 1960s institutional art world's apex of concern with art and technology. Jasia Reichardt's show *Cybernetic Serendipity* at the Institute of Contemporary Arts in London saw itself as "a reportage of current trends and developments."[23] The catalog included a history of digital computers; the exhibition placed work by Bridget Riley next to computer-generated graphics made by engineers.[24] The show took place in a 6,500-square-foot gallery and was seen by more than sixty thousand people.

Jasia Reichardt's discussion of *Studies in Perception* in *The Computer in Art* is both matter of fact and intensely ambivalent, stating that

> neither Knowlton nor Harmon sought an image that would be either abstract or synthetic, or indeed invented or in any way transformed. Quite rightly they considered that a common recognizable image would be the best vehicle to demonstrate the technique they had invented. On the other hand, their aim was also to produce something in the idiom of "modern art."[25]

These descriptions hedge their bets—"computer graphics," "computer art," "the technique they had invented," "in the idiom of modern art." They do not say what this image is or what it means but pronounce instead: something not entirely unlike art is on display here. This rhetoric foreshadows the problems that would later ensue between artists and engineers, museums and industry.

The term *computer art* announced serious problems. For modernist art, an attention to the specific materiality of the work was requisite to any serious critical discussion. According to a commonplace reading of Clement Greenberg, the ultimate goal of advanced art was to isolate and develop the specificity of its medium. The term *computer art* might seem on the surface to offer a material specificity, but it offers no such thing. *Studies in Perception* stands in, emblematically, for a larger transformation within the critical understanding of postwar aesthetics—the movement away from the object and toward a surrounding, encompassing context.

Looking at *Studies in Perception* in the context of Pontus Hultén's 1968 show at the Museum of Modern Art, *The Machine as Seen at the End of the Mechanical Age*, makes these stakes more evident, through the clear disjunctions between this and other works. As the title indicates, *The Machine as Seen at the End of the Mechanical Age* largely looks backward to the technology of the mechanical age at a moment when "the mechanical machine—which can most easily be defined as an imitation of our muscles—is losing its dominating position among the tools of mankind; while electronic and chemical devices—which imitate the processes of the brain and the nervous system—are becoming increasingly important."[26] The exhibition is dominated by mechanics—gears and wheels and representations of gears and wheels, functional and non, from Leonardo da Vinci's flying machines, to Marcel Duchamp's bachelor machines, and to Jean Tinguely's self-destructing machines.

However, there is also a set of works proposed by Experiments in Art and Technology (E.A.T.). The works associated with E.A.T are somewhat apart from the others, but perhaps less than one might think. They do have their own category in the show catalog, alongside other categories such as *art, reconstruction, invention, car,* and *camera*. But the E.A.T-categorized works are mostly sculptural and kinetic—in short, largely mechanical. Even among these, Knowlton and Harmon's work stands out as the only work in the show that mentioned computation as part of its process. The *Machine* show's iconography looked forward to the developments of the computer age, in part, by steadily focusing on the mechanized development of the past. The show fused art and design, including objects that are not art but are nevertheless allowed into the institutional embrace of the museum. The show recognized the importance of experimentation with computation but was unsure how to fit this work into the purview of the art world.

Unsurprisingly, the catalog is not clear on what to say about Knowlton and Harmon's work. It does not provide a visual description or an account of the encounter with the work. Instead, there is this statement:

> Computer graphics were created for utilitarian purposes. Among the uses are to study the field of view seen from the pilot's seat in an airplane, or to analyze a flat image in order to manipulate graphic data. The characteristics of the computer at the moment are strikingly shown in "computer art." The computer can act as an intelligent being: process information, obey intricate rules, manipulate symbols, and even learn by experience. But since it is not capable of initiating concepts, it cannot be truly creative; it has no access to imagination, intuition, and emotion.[27]

The author of this description is interested in the purposes of computer graphics, the uses and characteristics of the computer, and its possibilities and limitations in comparison to the human. The essay does not reference then-contemporary experimentation in the visual arts but, rather, "utilitarian" experiments in science and technology. "Computer art" is placed in quotations and is set apart from a larger field of artistic practice. It is understood to be an intervention into the then-contemporary understanding of the characteristics of the computer rather than into a field of conceptual pop or op art. In several different ways, this description situates this as a work that is art and even image only secondarily, in a sideways fashion.

With the advent of the electronic circuit, technology is no longer shaped by push and lever, gear and wheel. Instead, it begins to be comprised of machines whose functioning is no longer, strictly speaking, visible, at least in the ways in which the technology of the machine era had been visible.[28] These new machines operate at a level of essentially invisible forces.[29] They operate on the level of transistors and resistors, diodes and gates. They operate on the level of the circuit board, whose electronic pulses are not visible to the naked eye. *Studies in Perception* presents a strange doubled vision, an intersection of pictoriality and encoding. It pushes us to question what is at stake in using this language of equations and circuit diagrams to disrupt a photographic image, which in the 1960s was increasingly associated with a machine aesthetic. *Studies in Perception* takes this aesthetic and filters it neatly through computer processing. The shifting of machinic paradigms emerges only as an afterimage.

Both the pleasures and the pains of photography hold in its status as a mechanical apparatus belonging to the nineteenth-century age of the industrial machine. This status is at the heart of its claims of indexicality, which were easily extended to cinema. Writing in 1971 in *Artforum*, Hollis Frampton called cinema "the Last Machine" and said that "it is customary to mark the end of the Age of Machines at the advent of video.... I prefer radar, which replaced the mechanical reconnaissance aircraft with a static, anonymous black box."[30] Radar, with its invisible operations, belongs to the era of the electronic circuit, the circuit board, and computation: it introduced a paradigm shift.

This paradigm shift was recognized at the Museum of Modern Art far earlier than the *Machine* show. Arthur Drexler had introduced the circuit board for the IBM 305 RAMAC (Random Access Memory Accounting system) into MoMA's collection in 1958, and it was presented that year in an exhibition of twentieth-century design. The RAMAC circuit board—a fascinating conflagration of wires held in a small metal box—also appeared as the last image in a catalog associated with this show, under the heading "The New Machine Art." Drexler explained in the catalog that the circuit board exemplified the shift from the industrial age of machines to the postindustrial era of computation. He stated that

Since the end of World War II electronics has altered our conception of how things need to be shaped in order to work, and of how they may be related to each other. Geometric machine art suggested by its finite shapes the direct action of push and pull: the new machines are incomprehensible unless one knows about the existence of invisible forces.... Perhaps the most striking characteristic of the new machine aesthetic is its dematerialization of finite shapes into diagrammatic relationships. Examples are the printed electrical circuits, which replace three-dimensional objects with groups of patterns printed on a flat surface. Such patterns can hardly be said to have precise boundaries, or to be complete in themselves.[31]

Not surprisingly, this maps the same transition that the later *Machine* show would—the transition from machines that visibly mimic or extend the gestural actions and functions of the human body to those that operate invisibly. As Felicity Scott points out, it indicates a "crisis of object brought about through electronics."[32] Drexler later stated, in explaining the status of the circuit board in the collection, that "It symbolizes the changing sense of what constitutes an object, the move from the finite geometry of the 20's and 30's which seemed to mark the ultimate development of the machine, to what has happened since the war with the development of electronics: the dematerialization of objects, the reduction to parts."[33] This characterization of "dematerialization" is particularly interesting, given the obdurate materiality of the object in question: it is not a printed circuit board or a minute storage disk but is bright orange wires and silvery metal. There is nothing dematerialized about this object—except in the nonvisibility of its larger relationships. Without the larger machine, it is utterly nonfunctional, and even with the larger machine, its functionality is invisible. Instead of objects with defined lines and precise limits— the pulley, the lever, the geared wheel—these are objects without clear-cut boundaries that are incomplete as simply themselves. They are partial objects or dependent objects, with all the uneasiness that attaches to that idea. And in the end, the *Studies in Perception* are resolutely partial, engaged in an interrogation of visibility and invisibility that was very familiar to an art world concerned with precisely those problems as the central problems raised by computer technology.

Between Vector and Pixel

The *Studies in Perception* are a reflexive interrogation of the capabilities of the S-C 4,020 and its status as an apparatus that was designed to make clear and legible what otherwise would remain unseen and invisible. Their interrogation wound up in the realm of avant-garde art rather than in the more obvious realm of science and engineering, where Julesz's works were more comfortably situated. *Nude*'s interrogation of perception was staged in the literal and figurative idiom of pop art, thus inserting "computer visualization" as a central term within a broader conversation about representation in late modern aesthetics.

But their work also was important for the question of computer graphics in the realm of science and engineering. Knowlton and Harmon wrote a paper based on their experiments with the S-C 4020 that argued for the utility of picture processing by computer on two fronts in particular—generation and transformation. Generation is all about making previously impossible things. Data becomes picture, rendering an invisible real-world phenomenon visible. Or an abstract algorithm is used to synthesize a picture, creating something unexpected. Under transformation, they listed two types—picture to abstraction (in which something is measured and recognized) and picture to picture (in which some transformation is made).

The possibilities that they suggest for the transformation of pictures read like Photoshop, only circa 1970—smoothing, edge detection, sharpening, abstraction, distortion, and rearrangement. They show examples of "computer-processed pictures" that look like contemporary Photoshop jobs: real-world objects are rendered brighter and clearer, and compression techniques abstract the essential information from the redundant. These are described as common and useful.

They discuss their work—which they show as a snip from a photo of a gargoyle next to its micropattern sibling—as a way to "develop new computer languages which easily and quickly manipulate graphical data, to examine some aspects of human pattern perception, and to explore new art forms."[34] But in contrast to the other photographic or graphical images, it seems to show the transition from point to square that characterized early bitmapped computer screens. Knowlton called his work an independent invention of the pixel, and looking at this particular image, he seems to be far from wrong. Although the original image of Deborah Hay was sampled as "points" by the flying point scanner, it is rendered as little squares to be produced by the Charactron screen. BEFLIX imagined what was essentially a grid of faux pixels before bitmapping was a commonsense ploy, enacting in the process the tension between two different conceptualizations of the pixel—as a point and as a square.

As Richard F. Lyon explains in his history of the pixel, the term was popularized in the 1970s, as a contraction of the words "picture element," but it was initially introduced in English in 1927 as a description of the "mosaic of dots" that comprised television.[35] He traces the lineage back further—to Germany, where in 1874 Paul Nipkow filed a patent for a mechanical scanning television in which he referenced Bildpunkte—literally "picture points" but now generally translated as pixels. In other words, the word *pixel* has a complex history in media forms other than the computational. In computation, it came to popularity with the development of a technology called *bitmapping*—a technology that produces a screen image one square at a time. Initially, one bit of memory was mapped to a single pixel—marking this pixel as either "off" or "on." This takes the binary code of the computer—its either/or nature—and ties it to a two-dimensional grid. Any given image is understood as a uniform grid of colored squares.

What often goes unstated is that the pixel emerges at the crux of the problem of translation between overlapping systems that are never entirely compatible—an artifact of the intersection of analog and digital technologies, of numerical notation stored in binary bits and screen images marked in light. It moves, sometimes awkwardly, between television and the computational, between projected and reflected light, between camera sensor and photo printer. In fact, the ontology of the pixel lies in this movement between sampling, storage and viewing. Alvy Ray Smith at Microsoft memoed his colleagues in 1995 that "A Pixel Is Not a Little Square! A Pixel Is Not a Little Square! A Pixel Is Not a Little Square!"[36] Hyperbolic protestation to clarify his understanding that for computer imaging a pixel is a point—the outcome of a process of sampling by which an analog image, continuously representational, becomes discrete. The squares emerge, as Smith indicates, as the repetition of a sampled point through a box filter. The squares of the "digital grid" are thus the outcome of a mode of filtering, tied to the processing and memory limitations of computational technology—but these squares also mark the development and refining of an ontology that simultaneously shapes and transgresses particular material technologies.

The micropatterns of *Studies in Perception* do not merely highlight the importance of diagrams for early computer graphics as a language. They also point toward the development of a screen that would be based not around lines and vectors but around tiny squares and grids and toward a world where the photographic and the computational would be intimately linked.

Between 1964 and 1970, Stan VanDerBeek worked with Kenneth Knowlton at Bell Labs to create a set of computer animations using the S-C 4020. Knowlton and VanDerBeek made eleven animations, ten of which were collected in a series called Poemfields. *The series was directly inspired by the S-C 4020. Poemfields is invested in the look of language; like concrete poetry, it edges between word and image. The S-C 4020s matrixed screen of letters—the graphic display of the Charactron—drew VanDerBeek to create a double vision of text and image, code and picture.*

Considered together, these works display a concern with the ways in which computational technology seemed to be at the verge of transforming our understanding of both pictorial representation and linguistic communication "at the close of the mechanical age." Working through language, VanDerBeek envisions the computer as a source and control mechanism for a new universal picture language that can confront a crisis of visibility and connection by means of a newly mobilized spectatorship based on the modulation of an immersive, ever-changing world-image stream.

An Image Machine

Stan VanDerBeek did not arrive at Bell Labs as a scientist or engineer. He came to the New Jersey campus in 1964 with an ambiguous title—artist-in-residence—and no clearly defined role to play. Like composer James Tenney before him, he did not fit with the main business of Bell Labs. Tenney described his own position in the lab as "something of an anomaly;

it was not made explicit to the higher levels of the administration what I was really doing."[1] But the late 1950s and 1960s had ushered in a new era of cooperation and communication between artists and engineers, and even if the upper-level administration did not understand what, exactly, he was supposed to be doing there, VanDerBeek was eager to take advantage of the technology available at a place like Bell Labs.

After studying modern architecture and design at the Cooper Union for the Advancement of Science and Art in New York and at Black Mountain College in North Carolina, VanDerBeek designed sets for a New York television station. By the mid-1950s, he was using the station's equipment to teach himself to make movies. His early film work used a hodgepodge of advertising images, newspaper clips, commercial film clips, magazine images, and other materials—anything and everything from the visual world around him. Slotting cutouts and drawings into an animation deck underneath a camera, he constructed elaborate assemblages frame by frame. These collaged animations never congealed into spatially coherent environments: perspective is perpetually out of whack, with objects frequently too large or too small for their surroundings. In *Science Friction* (1959), one of his best-known early works, technology ceaselessly makes and unmakes itself through the imagery of everyday newspaper stories and magazine advertisements. VanDerBeek's machines are always going wild, skewing between mundane, comic, liberatory, and disturbing in the space of a few frames. Newspapers become missiles, automobile tail fins agglomerate into rockets, and a television shows a brain injected by an enormous hypodermic before the screen is shattered by a rocket.

These early animated films won VanDerBeek awards and recognition and cemented VanDerBeek's place at the heart of New York's underground cinema scene. But VanDerBeek had always been interested in moving beyond the single image, and by 1963, he had started to create multiple-projection environments and events that used sound, still and moving images, film and, soon, video. VanDerBeek was nothing if not promiscuous with his materials – he referred to himself as "a migrant fruit-picker of technology."[2] Traditional film editing, yes, but also slides and audio experiments. Projectors on wheels that performers moved around a stage, slipping past dancers and musicians. A radio driving a drill bit. The hammers, nails and aluminum grain silo he used to construct a new film-in-the-round theater at his home in upstate New York. Essays, published in mainstream venues such as Time, Esquire, and Harper's Bazaar as well as more specialist venues, which read like a combination of prophetic science fiction, psychedelia-enhanced speculative metaphysics, and programming and production manuals.

At Bell Labs, VanDerBeek wanted to learn how to program a computer to make visual materials, but he was perhaps even more interested in the then-abstract future of worldwide communication networks—an interest spawned by his early association with Buckminster Fuller at Black Mountain College in the early 1950s. His instinct was that computers were the future for the arts and for everyday communication. Kenneth Knowlton, who signed on to teach him programming, commented that he and Van-DerBeek were "a superb example of the match-up that EAT (Experiments in Art and Technology) hoped to encourage."[3] When VanDerBeek arrived at the New Jersey campus of Bell Labs, he found a range of technologies—mainframe computers, transistors, audio samplers, and printers, all the equipment one might expect and more. But the machine that fascinated him was the S-C 4020 microfilm printer, which for an animation film-maker like VanDerBeek looked like nothing less than a technological breakthrough in film production technology.

The closed box at the center of the machine held an apparatus that would have been exquisitely familiar to him from his work with animated film—a camera angled to capture whatever was on the surface underneath it. But instead of a framed space for cutouts and drawings, there was a screen unlike anything he had seen before. The Charactron CRT, with that grid of 252 × 184 characters that produced not points of light but clear letters. In VanDerBeek's eyes, the S-C 4020 was a camera hooked up to a luminous printing press full of mobile letters that could switch positions, combine and recombine, and agglomerate into new shapes. Letters that potentially held the agility, the transformational restlessness of the cutouts of his previous films. No wonder he was enthralled with the possibilities. The letters of the Charactron inspired VanDerBeek to create a series he called *Poemfields*, which used letters and words to shape a graphic poetry that occurred in cinematic time. Visually, a double level of lettering structured the films: the smaller alphanumeric forms of the Charactron screen elements were used to build up the shapes of words. The use of language gestured, as well, to the layers of human and computer languages that went into the production of the film and the translation and compilation that occurred as different machines and parts of machines came into play.

The *Poemfields* animations were made using the S-C 4020, an IBM 7094 mainframe and Knowlton's TARPS language (Two-D Alphanumeric Raster Picture System), based on his earlier BEFLIX language. BEFLIX was a special-purpose programming language for film animation written in macro-based Fortran Assembly Protocol. TARPS was an even more specialized language that Knowlton developed for VanDerBeek out of BEFLIX. Like BEFLIX, it had only a few basic operations—drawing straight lines or curves, copying a region, moving a region, a solid fill, a zoom, and a dissolve. In 1970, VanDerBeek described making movies with this system for *Art in America* as an arduous process. A computer program is written "in this special language, and put on punched cards; the punched cards are then fed into the computer; the computer tabulates and accepts the instruction on the cards, calculating the explicit details of each implied picture of the movie and putting the results on tape."[4] The tape was then run on the S-C 4,020. In its sealed box, each sequenced frame lit up the screen in turn as the camera clicked forward in controlled increments. Programmed variations of the letters and numbers of the Charactron created the range of tones.

VanDerBeek was candid about the effort involved and the potential for time-consuming mistakes: "after much trial and error—during which time the computer informs you that you have not written your instructions properly—you have a black and white movie."[5] This black and white movie could then be edited and colorized traditionally or transformed with standard editing techniques by adding and repeating sections. Knowlton programmed the initial work in consultation with VanDerBeek. But within a few months, VanDerBeek became fairly proficient at the programming process and started coding his own films.[6] As Knowlton said elsewhere, "because of their high speeds of calculation and display, the computer and automatic film recorder make feasible the production of some kinds of films that previously would have been far too expensive or difficult."[7] For VanDerBeek, this was a revolution in the conception of film: "the artist is no longer restricted to the exact execution of the form; so long as he is clear in his mind as to what he wants, eventually he can realize his movie or work on some computer, somewhere."[8]

VanDerBeek called the series *Poemfields* in reference to the Charactron screen, which he understood as a mosaic field that orchestrated letters and characters. The result was an image organized as a blocky raster grid. Earlier computer animation, such as that produced by John and James Whitney, began with hand-drawn images and scored them by means of processing algorithms to produce dizzyingly organic images. John Whitney went on to make similar animations on mainframe computers at IBM, using vector screens to generate both straight lines and curves. These beautiful circular forms stood in sharp contrast to the formal constraints of early grid-based graphics. The Charactron balked at delicate curving lines but excelled at reproducing specific letters—which could then be used to create grids, gradients, and blocks.

In the *Poemfields*, numbers and letters were overlaid with hand-painted blocks of color. The result was a flickering field that combines perceptual elements into words and then dissolves them back into illegible noise. The techniques for creating these flickering mosaics were developed from images created by Béla Julesz and Carol Bosch for their experiments exploring depth perception and binocular vision.[9] These images used semirandom generation to create graphic noise "whose patterns were reflected several times to produce intricate mandala grids resembling Persian carpets and snowflake crystals."[10] In *Poemfields*, the simple building blocks of the Charactron give rise to intricate patterns that nevertheless retain a distinctive look, something not unlike a style. The image emerges from small squares, each a single, discrete unit. The squares are too large for an illusion of continuity, and the image takes on the look of a mosaic.

In a discussion of the media that he has used in his work, VanDerBeek argues that painting is constructed stroke by stroke and animation is made frame by frame. Computers, he claims, construct by turning "on and off" and assembling images "bit by bit."[11] VanDerBeek emphasized that the state-of-the-art graphics display systems of that time worked by integrating "small points of light turned on or off at high speeds. A picture is 'resolved' from the mosaic points of light." He related this process to that of the human eye, itself "a mosaic of rods and cones."[12] The *Poemfields* series, then, is meant to be a set of "pictures within pictures" or, perhaps more precisely, letters within language, with the result that these basic elements give rise to a perceptual field that is constantly dissolving and reforming before our eyes, insistently calling our attention to both the language that VanDerBeek is using and how it is pictured.[13]

In his 1970 book *Expanded Cinema*, Gene Youngblood describes the *Poemfields* as "computer films" or "cybernetic cinema." For Youngblood, these works are not really "films" at all but works of art that utilize the filmic substrate as part of a more complicated system.[14] Like Kenneth Knowlton and Leon Harmon's *Studies in Perception* series of computer-processed pictures, the *Poemfields* animations were created in a multilayered process that frustrates the idea of a singular material condition. *Poemfields* is a computer program, the process of that computer program within the machine, the visual readout of a tiny cathode ray tube (CRT) screen, and a color-enhanced 16 mm print whose carefully toned gelatin ticks steadily through a film gate, erasing the viewer's perception of any division between its serial images. *Poemfields* is concerned with the processing of languages and the appearance of language on a computer screen. This dual fascination with language—as system and as material form—showcases a concern with the layers of representation occasioned by computation and computerization. The *Poemfields* films already partake in the

Still from *Poemfield No. 2*, precolorization (1966).

aggregative interlocking supports and layered conventions of cinema. But added onto that is the layered, differential specificity of the S-C 4020 and the interlocking elements around it, ranging from the IBM 7094 to the card punch. Attending to this complex system complicates our understanding of computational materiality in this time period, but it also can offer a different perspective from which to approach the hybridity of contemporary computers.

A Poem Machine

Poemfield No. 2, from 1966, was built from the black and white film of the S-C 4020, imprinted with letters from the Charactron, and carefully colored by hand. It is a kaleidoscopic rush of words, pattern, and brilliant color. Incongruously, it begins with string instruments and cymbals, before blocked colorfields begin to spark and flicker in abruptly changing abstract patterns. Enigmatic words and partial conjunctions resolve out of an amorphous field before dissolving back into a mosaic of dedifferentiation. VanDerBeek's words dissolve into pattern and picture before morphing back into words. These words shift and mutate, fracture and fragment, to travel down the screen in a laconic calligraphy. The viewer reads them, but it is impossible not to *see* them as well: they remain shapes, images, pictures. Linguistic and pictorial representations morph and coalesce as words fuzz out into what would now be termed *pixilation* or *digital noise*. The color is psychedelic. The underscoring technology, computational. The presentation is cinematic. Yet the artist presents the work as, simply, a poem.

The questions of visibility and invisibility take on a particular resonance at this historical moment, a few years before the graphical user interface emerged as the standard form of computational interface. The operations of mainframe computers like the IBM 7094 had been essentially invisible. Most functions of the computer occur at a level of electronic circuits, whose state changes are impossible to see with the human eye. As Matthew Fuller reminds us, "it is worth noting that simply because they occur at the level of electrons the axes of software are impossible to find for the average user. Just as when watching a film we miss out the black lines in between the frames flashing past at 24 per second, the invisible walls of software are designed to remain inscrutable."[15]

And the graphical image, far from being the central interface for the computer, was peripheral. Pictures, line drawings, graphs: they were all add-ons to the mainframe. At the level of the interface, these mainframes were, more or less, language machines with language input for programs and printouts for output. The peripheral status of the image in computation in this time period renders any depiction of the layering of language, code, and pictoriality both suspect and complex, engaged in a near-fictional imagining of possibility. Exploring the forms that VanDerBeek and Knowlton created in their *Poemfields* series (1964–1970), the movement between language and picture speaks to a complicated chain of differing materialities. These works mine a terrain between visibility and invisibility, with the surface of the image appearing in a double vision of text and image, code and picture. These works tease the viewer by walking a fine line between legibility and illegibility.

Poemfield No. 2 begins in darkness, with a thrum of stringed instruments. A single word appears on the screen in a blaze of red, blue, teal, white, and pink, backgrounded with a pattern not unlike television static— *LIFE*. Suddenly the word *LIKE* flares underneath it, In a burst of pink, the words are rearranged—*LIFE LIKE*.

A transcription of the first half of the film reads as follows:

```
LIFE / LIKE / LIFE / LIKE / ALL / ARE

/ POEM FIELD

/ POEM FIELD
```

/ POEM FIELD

/ SIMILAR / LIKE / LOOK / CLOCK / TICK / TICK / WE / PICK
/ LIFE / OUT

Language here is command—*look*, *like*, *pick*. This is temporal; it is a process. *LOOK. CLOCK.* Seeing and seeming move in a space between subjects, between a we and a you that are simultaneously similar and different. The words, too, play in a space of similarity and difference. Words shift with a letter. *LIFE* becomes *LIKE*, becomes *LIFE LIKE*. Throughout *Poemfield No. 2*, phrases coalesce as the viewer intuitively searches for connection, for configuration—for a system of organization. *Life like* calls to mind the robot, the automaton. Cybernetic theory springs to mind, but then the poem ticks on. Order fragments; it is difficult not to lose track of potential semantic units. As the film goes on, it becomes apparent that this language is not transparent. It does not seem to plainly describe. It is not straightforwardly readable. The words do not signify ideation with any clarity. Instead, they slip from one to the next through particular schemes of sound and the play of signifiers. *LIKE* to *LOOK* to *CLOCK*. The word *SEEMING* is replaced by *TO SEE*, the second partially taken from the first. This syntax turns on relationality—of words, phonemes, and morphemes. Again, it is difficult to read this language; it insists on being looked at.

Halfway through the film, a burst of noise overtakes the frame. The screen is subdivided into a grid, and each of the grid's squares is then further subdivided. From this overall field, the word *OUT* emerges in a flare of pink that turns quickly to a burnout of white. The words *OR APART* fade in over. Transcribing *Poemfield No. 2* from the halfway point, it reads as follows:

OR / APART / SEEMING / TO SEE / SEPARATE / THINGS / TO-
GETHER / SO / YOU / SAY / IT / WOULD / SEEM / LIFE / LIKE
/ THIS / LIVING / BUT / WE / ALWAYS / SUSPECT / IT

Each word or phrase appears separately on the screen, fading or flickering out for the next. This cannot be read like a poem on a page, with the eye moving forward and backward across words that are visible all at once. These appear and disappear quickly, placing the viewer in the time of the film. The viewer is pushed to read at a particular pace, making reading into a looking that is increasingly machinic, increasingly automatic. The play of words, their similarity rather than their difference, and the nonnarrative structure make it hard to remember the precise phrasing on a single viewing. Instead, each grouping looks simultaneously forward and backward. What jumps out are themes—seeming and similarity, an analogy of appearances that the film insists on as minor variations make new words. New words but also new shapes.

What does VanDerBeek's language look like? This is the question we need to ask of works that so stubbornly insist on the appearance rather than the disappearance of linguistic materiality. When the word *OUT* appears, it is pure white—all colors or none, depending on whether it is viewed on film, on a liquid-crystal display (LCD) screen, or on a CRT tube. It is simultaneously absence and presence before it fills with color. The words *OR APART* emerge, and an enlarged section of the phrase appears behind it like a form of obscure hieroglyphics or Chinese ideograms. These partial letters and partial phrases scroll down the screen in green, blue, and red. In giving way to *TO SEE*, the word *SEEMING* flickers out in a luminous fog of white light, leaving a white space in the middle of the screen—blooming a hole into the field of representation. Pink and white, *SEEMING* flares back into place. Then another burnout. The screen is overtaken by a mosaic of blinking white, blue, and black pattern. This dark pattern gives way to language. Yet these words are shapes to be taken apart and pieced together in new ways.

Poemfield No. 2 catches, over and over, somewhere between visibility and nonvisibility. To look at this image is to look away from the language. The text of the film disappears if the viewer's attention is forced to the surface of the representation. The gradations of gray are formed by letters and numbers—keyboard characters that disappear as independent forms in most replications of the films. But in their original imagining, the viewer is called to attend to the surface of the image as it appears in a curious double vision—text and image, code and picture. The viewer is pushed to consider the translation from word to image to arrangement of characters—and the transformation from these characters to the binary digits that lie at the heart of digital representation. The viewer is invited to consider the process of computation as it participates in and is structured by a whole series of representational layers, both analog and digital.

Language here is hyperbolically visible and yet consistently dissolving into illegibility. The *Poemfields* films are based in the characters and letters of the S-C 4020 and vividly represent the particularities of this particular computer screen. The films in the *Poemfields* series vary in length and tone but are consistent in their surface pattern and texture and their concern with language. Their durational form, however, makes it difficult for the viewer to create meaningful syntactical units. It is impossible to give an impression of how it does this through a sequence of still images. Still images implicitly banish a large portion of the disruption that is at the heart of VanDerBeek's films. Stills cannot evoke the abrupt strobing shifts that mark VanDerBeek's language, the ways that it is shaped by flare—one color after another, frame by frame, shifting text and pattern.[16] It is impossible to see these colors distinctly—rather, one seems to feel them. The screen seems to expand and contract. The optical effect is hallucinatory, seductive.

Language, Structure, and System

At this moment in the 1960s, art was becoming explicitly concerned with language as never before,[17] and this turn to language was often accompanied by another word—*information* (as in information technology). Kynaston McShine called his survey of conceptual art at the Museum of Modern Art in New York *Information*, and Jack Burnham titled his show at the Jewish Museum in New York *Software, Information Technology: Its New Meaning for Art*, while Terry Atkinson and Michael Baldwin titled their influential essay on conceptual art "Information." As Eve Meltzer has noted, for the art of this period, "'information' signaled a scientistic aesthetic."[18] Whether explicitly as in Burnham or implicitly as in McShine, artists and curators were drawing inspiration from cybernetics and general systems theory—and the ever-encroaching culture of computerization. Language was front and center in these shows—not just in wall text and catalogs but in the matter of the work itself. Think of the bold text of Hans Haacke's *MoMA Visitor's Poll* (1970) or the block print of John Baldessari's *Painting for Kubler* (1969). The fear, as Oscar Morgenstern expresses in the catalog for the *Information* show at MoMA, was that "worldly images, pictures, measuring rods cannot cope with the world."[19] Words, not pictures, were necessary for an art that was considering a world remade by information technology.

Poets also were concerned with language and its materiality. "Concrete poetry" was a field that stressed visual appearance. For some critics, it was seen as relying on "quaint illustrational or pictorial modes ... out of touch with changing paradigms in the visual arts and the wider conditions of language in modernity."[20] But concrete poetry's fascination with the look of information was one it shared with much of the advanced art of the time. Although the founders of the movement—the Noigandres group in Brazil and Eugen Gomringer in Switzerland—were concerned with the visual element of the poem, concrete poetry, like the roughly contemporary movement of "information art," was also concerned with the visual structure of information, with how "graphic space acts as structural agent."[21]

In part, concrete poetry develops out of an engagement with the mathematical model of communication developed by Claude Shannon. Eugen

Gomringer telegraphs his intentions with a call for a universal poetry of "information and communication."[22] Max Bense, a teacher and mentor of the concrete poets in Europe, combined information theory, cybernetics, and Charles S. Peirce's semiotics to create what he termed "information aesthetics"—a formalist, mathematical theory of contemporary art that worked to quantify the ratios between order and chaos, information and redundancy. Bense viewed information theory as a means for reinventing both aesthetics and textuality by focusing on formal programming and algorithmic possibility.[23] In this model, language is interrogated as a system—a development that runs in parallel with structuralism. With Bense, this differentiation of meaning from language leads to a rematerialization of language. As the name suggests, language is here made concrete, material.

Gomringer stated in 1954 that contemporary languages were moving toward "formal simplification ... abbreviated restricted forms of language are emerging."[24] He calls this "the very essence of poetry ... the aim of the new poem is simple and can be perceived visually as a whole as well as in its parts. It becomes an object to be both seen and used ... its concern is with brevity and conciseness."[25] Gomringer goes on to say that a poem in this mode is memorable because it "imprints itself upon the mind as a picture."[26] He calls this picture, in which the basic unit is a word, a *constellation*: "it encloses a group of words as if it were drawing stars together to form a cluster ... In the constellation something is brought into the world. It is a reality in itself and not a poem about something or other."[27] Yet in addition to materiality, according to Gomringer, concrete poetry declares a fascination with structure and organization. It is concerned with concentration and simplification, brevity and conciseness, and communication. It resists semantics in favor of structure. Rosemarie Waldrop says, "we do not usually see words ... we read them, which is to say we look through them at their significance, their contents. Concrete Poetry is first of all a revolt against this transparency of the word."[28] This turn to the materiality of language often betrays a concern with system and information—and in this, a concern with the developing culture of computerization.

Prior to *Poemfields*, VanDerBeek's body of work consisted primarily of a practice of collage animation using cut-up magazines and other kinds of imagery, predominantly photographic.[29] He returned to this aesthetic throughout his career, but *Poemfield No. 2* contains only the faintest traces of it. Instead, it animates language—combining and recombining words.[30] Like other examples of concrete poetry, *Poemfield No. 2* forms constellations, drawing words together like stars.

VanDerBeek was not the only person experimenting with poetry and computers at this time, of course. Jackson MacLowe and Alison Knowles were both writing poems using mainframe computers. Following John Cage's popularization of chance operations, both used the computer primarily as an instigator for anti-intentional serendipity. Their poems were algorithmic experiments where the computer sutured together text in semirandom blocks. In contrast, VanDerBeek's language is directly authored by VanDerBeek without deliberate recourse to chance or randomness. But VanDerBeek's language play does join MacLowe and Knowles's work and differs from most language-based art and concrete poetry in that it was articulated through a cascading chain of human *and* machine-readable languages. An initial poem was turned into picture with the Fortran-based TARPS with the aid of the lettered screen of the S-C 4020.[31]

It is important to remember that at this point in 1968, the computer is, despite remarkable achievements by the Ivan Sutherlands and Douglas Engelbarts of the world, a thick concatenation of rather obdurate, exceedingly visible, difficult material. The IBM 7094 did not offer the experience of zooming through information space that Engelbart's NLS produced to the euphoric rapture of audience and users alike. Rather, the IBM 7094 was a room-sized pile of equipment that needed to be fed information with stacked and collated paper punchcards. Memoirs recount the complicated process of writing a program, transposing it to punchcards, running it, revising errors on a printout, and returning to reprint a stack of punchcards. Thus, to be concerned with the computer at this point was necessarily to be concerned with certain problems of translation and transposition. To be concerned with the computer at this point in time was to be concerned with the particularities of language—or languages.

Poemfield No. 2 calls us to pay attention to the material constraints—the materiality—of its production. Language is considered as an abstract representation of a self-referential linguistic world. Language takes its place not as it refers to objects but as it refers to itself as a system. Yet the visual model depends on the specific functioning of the programming language that is used to construct it. In this imaging, the visual structures of the individual words become clues to a structural arrangement. In debt to this structural arrangement within this perceptual field, language is reimagined as picture—a picture that is generated with a certain series of precise constraints.

This reimagining might seem a strange gesture because the computer at this point was more the domain of the linguistic than the pictorial. In fact, in examining the 1960s' turn to the linguistic, a newfound concern with computerization appears—especially a concern with the informational, cybernetic reorganization and reimagination of the world heralded by computerization. That these words often did not directly reference computation or filter through computational media is perhaps beside the point.

Like these experiments, VanDerBeek and Knowlton's work allows us to place the emergent field of linguistic aesthetics into dialogue with a nascent culture of computation. But VanDerBeek and Knowlton's language forms lack the studied visual neutrality or "scientistic" aesthetic that much of the new art involving language shared. VanDerBeek and Knowlton's language, unlike so many other interrogations, is deliberately disruptive to perception and unsteady on the screen, transforming itself through afterimages. This code-driven animation was quite different from the more traditional practices used by VanDerBeek in earlier films, and it offers us a contrary view of computation in this time period. The *Poemfields'* turn to a concretized language provokes an understanding of how media forms and practices can directly shape the bodies that interact with them, changing both what is seen and how we are able to see.

Reimagining Computation

In his *Understanding Media: The Extensions of Man*, Marshall McLuhan expounds on the idea of changing "sense ratios."[32] He claims that "the effects of technology do not occur at the level of opinions or concepts, but alter sense ratios or patterns of perception steadily and without any resistance."[33] Later, he states that "any invention or technology is an extension or self-amputation of our physical bodies, and such extension also demands new ratios or new equilibriums among the other organs and extensions of the body."[34] McLuhan associated the culture of the book with the dominance of the visual sense, and with the age of the electronic, he traced a return to a certain synesthesia. He argues that the new electronic media are multisensory and tactile: they envelope us and insist that we participate.

McLuhan's rhetoric of sensory expansion and transformation, visual learning, and a global information culture can suggest a somewhat uncomfortable sense of technological determinism. But he reserves a special role in this deterministic landscape for the artist. According to McLuhan, artistic practice can and should "exact information of how to rearrange one's psyche in order to anticipate the next blow from our own extended faculties.... In experimental art, men are given the exact specifications of coming violence to their own psyches from their own counter-irritants or technology."[35] The artist can correct the sense ratios for viewers—a call that VanDerBeek seems to have taken to heart when he claims in his 1959 essay "The Cinema Delimina: Films from the Underground" that he is interested in "abandoning the logics of aesthetics" and "springing full-blown into a juxtaposed and simultaneous world that ignores the one-point-perspective mind, the one-point-perspective lens."[36]

In *Poemfields*, the fusion of the haptic, optic, and auditory that McLuhan spoke of is readily apparent. It is a blend of dada and beat that practically anticipates the "glitch" aesthetics of a much later period. Here, VanDerBeek reimagines himself as a systems programmer who is working at the man-machine interface. Watching the film, the viewer is constantly disoriented as the gestalt caves from words to image and back. The experience of the disjunctive soundtrack, with its clashing of instruments, becomes another part of this. There is never a totalizing mode of vision where everything might be grasped and held in a single, mastering gaze. The film often seems to shudder, vibrating minutely with an uneasy tempo. This is due to the S-C 4020 as well. It did not initially come with stable vertical registration pins, so the picture subtly oscillates and shakes from frame to frame.[37] As the screen is destabilized, so too is the body of the spectator. This jitter combines with the psychedelic color to create a dislocative viewing experience. These moving images provoke a complex bodily engagement that results in a spectacular phenomenological disruption. They are experienced as aggressive, overwhelming, headache-inducing. They seem to provoke a "visual pain" in the average spectator.

VanDerBeek has taken the computer—an object tightly bound to cybernetics and systems theory, to command and control, to a technocratic rationale—and reimagined it as a representational space that provokes a complex and potentially overwhelming bodily affect. In its "concretized" language, there is a suspicion of the transparency that was necessary to the military operations of the radar screens that the Charactron was built for. Instead of transparency, there is a distinctive emphasis on the material constraints placed on representation.

In these images, VanDerBeek relies on the pictoriality of language. Computer code, in a complex cascade of representations, is situated in an equally complex relationship to the body. In the destabilization of the body of the spectator, the potential of technological control lingers. McLuhan's claims that a controlling power can be attributed to particular mediating technologies come to mind, especially in his insistence that in their function as extensions, these technologies reconfigure our bodies. In these films, VanDerBeek shifts traditionally understood ratios of haptic and optic. And indeed, the body of the spectator becomes a site where the computer code is activated. Yet as the flashes and flarings of the screen disrupt our perception, burning spectral images onto our retinas, they provoke us into a new understanding of the ways in which media forms and practices can gear directly into the body, bypassing rational understanding, shaping and remolding our perceptual apparatus, and changing what we are able to see.

After coming to Bell Labs, VanDerBeek began to reimagine the capacities of the computer in relation to graphic representation. To quote VanDerBeek: "computers came to my attention in 1965 with some of the graphic possibilities.... I consider the computer-logic systems and process of image making, a fast high speed car, that is difficult to learn how to drive."[38] The experience of driving a sports car: this is the metaphor VanDerBeek chooses in 1969, looking back to 1965, to describe both the computer logic systems and the process of image making. What does VanDerBeek mean? He reiterates the velocity of the computer—fast, high speed—as both its attraction and its difficulty. Yet it also is clear, in VanDerBeek's statement, with his reference to image making, that this velocity is intimately related to a new mode of picturing. Just as the machinic window of the automobile or the airplane implicitly frames a moving landscape into a picture, the computer, for VanDerBeek, is about a transformation in our ways of seeing.

VanDerBeek imagines his high-speed image machine as an extension of memory and as a new kind of printing press. He links personal memory and historical memory with the memory that is ensconced in the black box of the computer. "Memory," as VanDerBeek puts it in an earlier quote, "is the matrix of the human condition, and computers are the pertinent extension of the real-time-mind of man."[39] Later, he claimed that the computer was "a large black box: the memory of the world."[40] And finally, it was "a metaphysical printing press."[41] The relationship with the computer is here understood as capable of changing man's mind and, by extension, his sense of subjectivity.

Another Image Machine

Although there are eight films in the *Poemfields* series, numbered one through eight, they were not developed chronologically. They were created and edited at different dates, and VanDerBeek never seemed to understand any of them as finished works. The archives at the Museum of Modern Art in New York have several versions of each of the films, each marked by qualifiers such as "blue version" or "short version." In his essay on computer-animated films, Knowlton suggested that "the speed, ease and economy of computer animation permits the movie-maker to take several tries at a scene—producing a whole family of film clips—from which he chooses the most appealing result, a luxury never before possible."[42] VanDerBeek was accustomed to using and reusing material from his work in collage, but the possibilities of computer animation took this habit to another level, allowing him to run and rerun a sequence with minor variations rather than laboriously duplicating each by hand. The result is that there are no definitive versions of each film, only provisional iterations that exist in a process of reuse, transformation, and variation.

Even more important, VanDerBeek did not isolate these films as stand-alone works but saw them instead as potential sources of audiovisual material for his "Movie-Drome"—a screening space that he was creating from a grain silo. VanDerBeek began building the thirty-one-foot high aluminum Movie-Drome in 1963 and 1964 simultaneously with the *Poemfields* series. It was located near his home at the Gate Hill Coop, a community known as "The Land," where he lived alongside John Cage, Merce Cunningham, poet M. C. Richards, and others. VanDerBeek considered the Movie-Drome a prototype for a larger satellite-linked, real-time communication system in which individuals from around the world would be able to receive, recombine, and transmit audiovisual information from and to cities across the world.

VanDerBeek envisioned a computerized system that would remake cinema as a "performing art," implementing a universal picture language that was capable of educating large numbers of people both consciously and unconsciously. According to VanDerBeek, "the world hangs by a thread of verbs and nouns. Language and culture-semantics are as explosive as nuclear energy. It is imperative that we (the world's artists) invent a new world language ... that we invent a non-verbal international picture language."[43] This picture language was to incorporate potentially thousands of images at once, projected on a spherical dome. Viewers would lie on their backs at the edge of the dome, feet pointed toward the middle, falling into an "image-flow" that would suffuse their field of vision and reorder "their levels of awareness."[44] Found material was mixed with VanDerBeek's computer animation, newsreel footage, underground films, and images from current events. VanDerBeek hoped that this transformation would bring far-flung cultures together, in part by pushing people to understand the ramifications of technology. He stated that "technological research, development ... has almost completely out-distanced the emotional-sociological (socio-'logical') comprehension of this technology," but unlike others in this time period, he saw the solution to this as within the realm of technology.[45]

Poemfield No. 7, made collaboratively with John Cage, addressed Van-DerBeek's frustration with a military industrial complex built for war. It is arguably the most intricately patterned of all the films. The language seems to be moving even further toward pattern or picture, with closing credits that resolve into names only with great difficulty:

```
LOVES

OR

LOVES

OF

THERE

IS

NO

WAY TO

PEACE

PEACE

IS

THE WAY

NO MORE

WAR
```

The Movie-Drome for VanDerBeek was intended to serve as a "way to peace" by producing historical understanding and emotional empathy through a novel mode of audiovisual communication. VanDerBeek linked the *Poemfields* films to the Movie-Drome in a poster from 1966 that mixed stills from *Poemfields* with photos of the Movie-Drome. The print is structured as a series of rotating, interlocking grids, and VanDerBeek in the poster articulates his understanding of a parallel structure between the computer display system and the eye and between the computer and the mind. The text states that "the mind is a computer—not railroad tracks. Human intelligence functions at the order of 100,000 decisions p/second." Rotating counterclockwise: "The computerized graphic display system shown here in stills from the computer generated movie 'Poem Field No. 1' ... was 'drawn' at speeds of 10,000 points p/ second." Continuing counterclockwise: "The Present State of Design of Graphics Display systems: integrate small points of light turned on or off at high speeds. A picture ... is resolved from the mosaic points of light. The eye is a mosaic

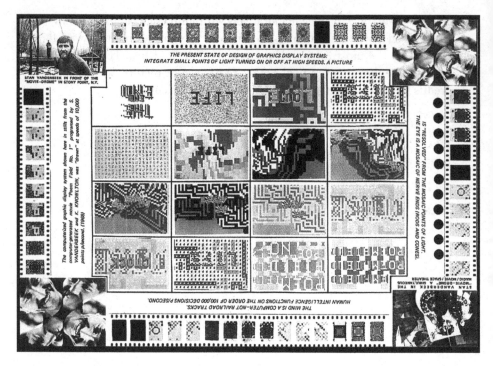

Poemfields poster (1966).

of nerve ends (rods and cones)." There is no prescribed way of reading the image, no up or down, left or right, but rather an intersection with an active, moving viewer.

In 1969, VanDerBeek was invited to show *Poemfields* at the Cross Talk Intermedia festival in Tokyo, an event designed to introduce computer music and experimental film to a wider public audience.[46] The three-day event, sponsored by Pepsi, Sony, TEAC, and the American cultural center, drew more than ten thousand visitors. VanDerBeek, flown over by the Rockefeller Foundation, adapted *Poemfields* to a much larger space than the Movie-Drome—the Yoyogi National stadium. Eight of the films were projected on portable screens, moved gradually around the stadium by assistants. The screens were followed by projectors on rolling carts, cutting bright beams of light across the space as they tried to match film to screen. The floor of the stadium, about two hundred feet in diameter, was freely traversed by the equipment but also by the spectators, who were encouraged to move around by open seating.

The movement between the intimacy of the Movie-Drome and the sprawl of the stadium shows the complicated intermediate space of art and technology that VanDerBeek inhabited. To produce and show the *Poemfield* films, VanDerBeek moved between the do-it-yourself space of the Gate Hill Coop and the multimillion-dollar equipment of Bell Labs and between the sites of experimental film, music and art, and commercial technology. In doing so, he made works that were provisional and tactical, geared to the constraints of a particular moment, even as they were unfinished, moving hopefully into the future.

From Language to Image

Throughout the 1960s and 1970s, there was a tension between the conceptualization of the computer as, on the one hand, a code-based machine for textual communication and, on the other, a screen-reliant space of pictorial representation. VanDerBeek and Knowlton's work in the *Poemfields* series articulates a conception of the representational space of the computer that is both anticipatory and alternative. Over a decade before Hollis Frampton's better-known computer experimentation, Stan VanDerBeek was concerned with the ways in which computational technology seemed to be at the verge of transforming our understanding of both pictorial representation and linguistic communication. The central characteristics of the S-C 4020 critically shaped the creation and viewing of the *Poemfield* series. As stated earlier, the S-C 4020 was a language machine, which gave VanDerBeek cause to consider language as an element of the moving image in a way that he had not previously done. In using this machine, he came to understand code as both the building blocks of a film and a database for images thought more generally. VanDerBeek called it "an abstract notation system for making movies and image storage and retrieval systems."[47]

In *Poemfields*, VanDerBeek is engaging with the S-C 4020 as a platform, a site for representation that allows him to question what representation might become in the era of the digital computer. This interrogation brings the hybridity of the computer systems of this era—how they stood intertwined, rather than separate—into sharp relief. In the 1970s, there were two threads for computer graphics—the linear vector graphics of the point-plotting screen and an emergent screen of bitmapped graphics. The blocky characters of *Poemfields* point toward the bitmapped screen and the ways in which pictorial representation would allow computers to become ever more thoroughly integrated into the spectatorial body.

By 1971, when Lillian Schwartz made her film Pixillation, *Bell Labs was beginning to slide from the cutting edge of research and development and cede this position to the West Coast and Silicon Valley. The art and technology movement publicly imploded with an ill-received show at the Los Angeles County Museum of Art (LACMA), at which artists were accused of collaborating with a sprawling military-industrial complex that was seemingly impervious to critique and that continued to occupy Southeast Asia. By 1972, Xerox PARC would boot up the Alto, arguably the first personal computer, and initiate an eclipse of the mainframe era.*

This chapter focuses on Pixillation, ENIGMA, UFO's, *and* Googolplex— *films that Schwartz made at Bell Labs with Kenneth Knowlton and others. At a time when medium specificity was in full retreat within the contemporary art world, Schwartz's works developed a unique computational aesthetic through their engagement with the medium of the microfilm plotter. As a group, these works perform an extended interrogation of the capabilities and limitations of S-C 4020 as an abstracted platform. Beginning with* Pixillation's *strikingly hybrid intermedia innovation in the face of material constraint, these films progress toward the structurally rigorous* Googolplex, *an ascetic experiment in which the solitary modulation of black and white strives to generate an experience of flaring color for the spectator. In dialogue with both structural film and the video art of the period, the progression of these works evidences an analytics of reduction and constraint in which hand-drawn animation, color filters, and even color processing are all stripped from her practice. With* Googolplex, *she arrives at a generative serial composition that explores the process of seeing itself*

*with a stark aesthetic that probes the capacities of the microfilm plotter—a swan
song for a technology whose days were numbered.*

The End of the Mechanical Age

In 1968, several major museum shows addressed the relationship between
art and technology in order to interrogate its philosophical stakes. Exhibi-
tions took up machinic art but also art made with the new computational
machines that were then transforming the corporate and scientific landscape. Pontus Hultén's 1968 show at the Museum of Modern Art (MoMA),
The Machine as Seen at the End of the Mechanical Age, was one show that
marked this transition from mechanical equipment to informational
technologies. The show primarily looked backward at gears, levers, and
wheels—taking stock of a century of mechanical devices to understand the
new era of computation that was just coming into focus. Necessarily, art
made with these new computational machines was included—but not
much of it. What "new" technology appeared in the exhibition was sup-
plied primarily by Experiments in Art and Technology (E.A.T.). The organization created by Robert Rauschenberg and Billy Klüver held a
competition for artworks created by the intentional collaboration of professional artists with professional engineers. The resulting works generated images out of process and performance, moving parts and audience
interactivity. Of 160 pieces originally entered into the competition, Hultén
selected nine for inclusion in MoMA's official show.[1]

Lillian Schwarz's kinetic sculpture *Proxima Centauri* was one of
these. From a distance, the work appeared austere: it was a highly pol-
ished, fifty-five-inch black pedestal. But the shiny box housed a complex
array of moving parts. There was a translucent dome, lit with constantly
changing abstract patterns. There were rods to move the dome, a slide
projector, a ripple tank, motors, and other assorted electronics. The work
was activated by pressure sensitive pads, and as viewers approached, it
came alive. A glowing dome rose out of the box, illuminated by a constantly
changing stream of abstract patterns. The exhibition catalog described the
dome as transforming into a kind of "a gelatinous mass that shakes,
breathes."[2] As viewers moved closer, the dome turned red and retreated
into the pedestal, inviting viewers to come closer still—until standing
nearly above it, they could peer down into its concealing base. Highly
dependent on the specificity of the viewer's actions, it was a work that
quite literally appeared differently to each individual viewer. Schwartz's
machine was a study in observation, contingency, and perspective whose
interactive modulations of color and luminosity required a tricky bit

of engineering. This last part was greatly aided by Schwartz's E.A.T.-engendered connection to the engineer Per Bjorn and sold her on the benefits of this kind of collaboration.[3]

Schwartz began as a painter trained in traditional Japanese brushwork. As a sculptor, she had initially cast bronze. But she traded a few of those early pieces to a factory owner for the opportunity to work with a decidedly more modern material—plastics. The material—all translucence and fascinating malleability—delighted her. She used catalysts to delay its setting time and rubber tubing to introduce bubbles into the casting process. The factory owner was bemused for "bubbles, of course, are the one thing plastics factories are constructed to avoid."[4] After the sheets had hardened, she used them as three-dimensional canvases, scoring them with blow torches, solvents, and drill bits. The results were simultaneously organic and industrial—a scrim of aerated waves and more mechanical imprints hovering in a ghostly three dimensions.[5]

Later, with works such as *World's Fair*, Schwartz pursued this formal interest in liquidity by introducing literal fluids into her sculpture. Mechanical elements controlled the flow of multicolored liquids as they passed through plastic tubing. She constructed metal boxes as frames for these sculptures, fixing the glass cylinders inside in varying arrangements. A slim vertical glass container held a separate spiraling tube, with the outer shell holding one color of liquid and the plastic tubing another. As the motors pushed and pulled liquids of varying colors and distinctive viscosities through the tubes, luminous and unexpected interactions arose. A pale orange might hold a tube of burgundy, or turquoise liquid might swirl through gold, creating a green shimmer. She had built the prototype with a Kenner toy set, but as she continued working in this vein, she developed more advanced electronic and mechanical devices that could precisely control both the flow of the liquids and their lighting.[6] Schwartz called these sculptures "fluid boxes," and like *Proxima Centauri*, their durational structure was an important forerunner to her films.

Seen from a distance, *Proxima Centauri*'s exterior geometry, like that of the fluid boxes, was clean and minimal. But while minimalist sculpture of the time was famously hollow—what you see is what you get—Schwartz's minimal surfaces were lures, concealing complex machineries that used both mechanics and electronics to generate a dazzling array of fluid forms. The appropriate reference is less minimalism than psychedelia, especially the psychedelic light shows that emerged out of the expanded cinema of the mid-1960s and became increasingly popular accompaniments to all manner of live musical performance. Like these, *Proxima Centauri* was a less a sculptural "specific object" than a dynamic, multimedia environment—one constantly changing for each spectator.

Within *The Machine as Seen at the End of the Mechanical Age*, Schwartz's sculpture was placed in the same room as the other works from the E.A.T competition. When visiting the exhibition, she became increasingly taken with another work in the room—an image of a reclining nude composed from distinct black and white micropatterns. She described it as "much like a photograph reproduced in a newspaper" but with an important difference: the image shifted and reformed itself as she moved toward or away from it or changed her viewing angle.[7] Despite not being an animated image, "it had a sense of animation," the kind of animation that she worked to generate in her own practice of drawing and sculpture.[8] Looking at it, she moved back and forth, "visually translating the nude into an abstract of black, grays and whites," and decided that this art needed a name. "Technological pointillism!" she exclaimed.[9] "No," a voice behind her answered. "That's Deborah Hay, the dancer. We processed her."[10] The voice was Leon Harmon, who had created the image at Bell Labs with Kenneth Knowlton. It was part of their *Studies in Perception* series, the computer-processed pictures they had made with an elaborate scanning procedure using the IBM 7090 and the S-C 4020. Harmon liked Schwartz's work and thought that she might be interested in the possibilities of the computers he and Knowlton were using.

His instincts proved correct. Harmon invited Schwartz to tour Bell Labs in Murray Hill, New Jersey, and it would be decades before she really left. For the next twenty years, Schwartz was a "resident visitor" at the Labs, and in its Acoustical and Behavioral Research Center, she made some of the most important computer art of the 1970s and 1980s. She worked there consistently but not always in an official capacity.[11] She started out by coming in at night because it allowed her to access the computers more easily. But eventually, she became a fixture within the enormous lab and was commissioned to make films and sculptures that pushed the boundaries of what was then possible with computer-graphic technology.[12] Laboratory director Max Mathews initially introduced her as the lab's "morphodynamicist," but she later took an official, proper, paid position as "consultant in computer graphics."[13]

Under Max Mathews and John R. Pierce, Bell Labs was a unique place to work. In the heyday before the divestiture, it was described as an idealized version of the ivory tower—something like a university research center but with even more openness and freedom. Researchers did not have to compete for grant money or fuss with administrative committees. Bell Labs hired the best and brightest PhDs coming out of university science and engineering programs, and they then largely left them alone to pursue their own idiosyncratic interests, by themselves or in collaboration with one another. The building's design separated offices and laboratories, so research staff constantly trekked between the two. Doors were generally open, and if people had a question about, say, information theory, they could walk a few doors down and simply ask one of the experts in the field. Equations might be drawn on a chalkboard, explanations given, and then everyone went back to their work with the renewed sense that each enterprise was somehow a communal one. Under Bell Lab's umbrella of long-term "research and development," proximity encouraged collaboration and cross-disciplinary inquiry.[14] And like much of the work discussed in the prior chapters, Schwartz's work is unthinkable outside of such collaboration. Kenneth Knowlton is cocredited on many of her films, but she also worked with other people at the Labs in creating them.

Under the auspices of Max Mathews, the Acoustical and Behavioral Research Center encompassed a range of experimental composers. Speech, of course, was the historical purview of Bell Laboratories, and it had an obvious interest in figuring out how to meld analog telephony and digital computing. Mathews had initially been assigned to figure out how to navigate speech and computers, beginning with the question of how to input speech or sound more generally into a computer, how to process it in various ways, and then how to play it back. Mathews interpreted this mandate broadly, and soon a coterie emerged at the Labs whose work was not confined to electronic sound but spilled over into computer music. The pairings were the peculiar ones that Bell Labs seemed to foster. Avant-garde musicians (such as John Cage, Edgard Varèse, Emmanuel Ghent, and Laurie Spiegel) became regular visitors at the Labs, and James Tenney became a staff member, working alongside physicists and mathematicians. As a result of this proximity, Schwartz's films were scored by respected computer musicians, including Gershon Kingsley (*Pixillation*), Emmanuel Ghent (*UFO's*), Richard Moore (*Enigma*), Jean-Claude Risset (*Mutations*), and Max Mathews (*Olympiad* and *Papillons*).[15]

"What we now know as computer art began in December 1968, [with] Lillian Schwartz," Nobel Laureate Arno Penzias later recounted: "Those who worked with her in those days still remember her monumental ingratitude to technology. As each problem was solved and each new capability came into hand, a new round of probing explorations would begin and off she would be, asking for the impossible all over again."[16] At the lab, Schwartz was generally appreciated for her unwillingness to accept traditional boundaries and for her insistence on pushing the limits of the technologies she employed.

A New Language

When Schwartz came to Bell Labs in 1968, John Vollaro, a technical staff member under Leon Harmon, taught her how to use the computer. "He began by patiently explaining the underlying concepts, the hows and whys of bits, transistors, processing units, and cathode ray tubes," but Schwartz found it difficult to pay attention, enraptured as she was by the arrays of lights flickering off and on, off and on. It was like Times Square at night, she thought,

> when the neon signs flickered with such intensity that my eyes would rapidly tire, casting an unfocused halo around the colors. I thought of Seurat's *petit point*, a style "where the continuous form is built up from the discrete, and the solid masses emerge from an endless scattering of fine points—a mystery of the coming-into-being for the eye."[17]

She longed to use the machine to make similar shimmering color-ations, with form emerging out of the smallest elements. At the lab, she initially began to work on a sequence of images done with Knowlton's BEFLIX. She showed the stages of the process in an early project from 1968. A drawing was made on paper. It was then transliterated into symbols. In keeping with what Knowlton understood to be the affordances of the S-C 4020, the output was letters from the alphabet and basic numbers. These were Schwartz's compositional elements as offered by BEFLIX. Each gridded square could be filled by one of the sixty available symbols, each capable of generating a certain level of brightness and thus a sem-blance of gray-scale spectrum from the available patterns.[18]

Schwartz described her initial work with BEFLIX and the S-C 4020 as "blind": there was not any "immediate interaction among input, an image appearing on a monitor, manipulation of the image, and output."[19] Because she was not transposing photographic images, as Harmon and Knowlton had, every element of an image had to be laboriously imagined and calcu-lated point by point, coordinate by coordinate. After the image was planned, the information was punched onto cards to be fed into the com-puter. There were two sets of cards—"one for the operations to be per-formed and the other for the assigned level of brightness for each symbol."[20] According to Schwartz, the keypunching itself was yet another layer of blindness: "it was easy to make a typing mistake and, unless one wanted to memorize the coding associated with the placement of each hole, [it was] difficult to detect the error until the final output."[21]

After the cards were punched, they went to the card reader. But again, blindness: it was impossible to see immediately what the cards had amounted to. They were output to magnetic tape. Schwartz then unhitched the tape from the card reader and carted it to another room. There she pushed the tape onto another drive, where it directed the microfilm printer to generate 35 mm black and white film, in either positive or negative. Only after the resulting film was developed could Schwartz finally see the images she had laboriously produced. She emphasizes the frustration of waiting for two or three days between "all of the tedious keyboard work" and the final output, the need to rigorously plan and previsualize everything beforehand, but also the potential that such a non-real-time apparatus afforded for both error and the wonder of surprise.[22]

Still—the more she learned about the BEFLIX system, the more exasperated she became with it. Stan VanDerBeek had looked at the S-C 4020 and envisioned a language made out of language. The innards of the machine looked like the editing tables he was familiar with and led him to envision a metaphysical printing press. Knowlton and Harmon were trained programmers interested in scanning photographs and saw the possibilities the computer offered for transcoding images through processing. Schwartz was neither an animator used to working in film nor a computer programmer. She did not have any particular preconceptions about the S-C 4020; she simply had to learn to work with it. Her descriptions make it clear that, on some level, she wanted immediate feedback— an interactivity that would allow her to emulate the nuanced control over materials she had possessed with painting and sculpture. Later innovations in graphics eventually allowed her to return to something like this. But at this point in her career, she was confronted with a device that, at least initially, offered possibilities and limitations almost entirely incommensurate with her prior training. As such, she was forced to explore the apparatus, constantly revising her habits and affinities. Instead of instantaneous response and graphic control, she was confronted with a staggered temporality and unanticipated effects. As a result, she pushed the graphic and representational possibilities of the IBM computer and its microfilm plotter to their limits and beyond.

Initially, Schwartz tried replacing the standardized computer-generated symbols in BEFLIX with intricate hand-drawn patterns. But she seemed inherently to feel that Knowlton had not pushed the limits of the instruments he was using—and that the best way to push those limits was to drill down into the particularities of the equipment. Initially, she focused on the blindness that the system engendered for her. She wanted to turn this procedural "blindness" to her advantage, and she sought to do so by creating something generative—an initial image and a process by which it could be transformed. This suggests that the surprise she experienced in discovering what her lengthy process of programming had entailed was not, for her, an ancillary affect to be cast off after the final creation had been given form. For Schwartz, the final result was bound up with the fickle and unpredictable process of creation itself—the surprise and even shock that it could offer. Her films were crafted to maintain this surprise within her audience's experience of the work. She labored to create effects that were unpredictable not just to her but to viewers. The blindness of the process drove her to create generative films where the accident—the bug, as she termed it—was an ineluctable part of the structural affordances of the system.

Knowlton had used the BEFLIX program with Harmon to generate the *Studies in Perception* series and with VanDerBeek to create the groundbreaking *Poemfields* series of animated films. Working with Schwartz, however, he became increasingly conscious of the program's limitations. As Knowlton acknowledged, BEFLIX was not designed for presentation of "artistic material."[23] In the process of working with Schwartz, he began to feel that the language was "scientifically oriented" and that it would be possible and desirable to develop languages that were more suited to artistic production, more specifically designed for use by professional artists.

In the process of working with Schwartz on her film *Pixillation*, Knowlton developed EXPLOR (Explicit Patterns, Local Operations, and Randomness).[24] Like BEFLIX, EXPLOR was a macro language program written with the Bell Labs macro Fortran Assembly Program.[25] And like BEFLIX, EXPLOR structured the screen by dividing it into a grid of pixels, an innovation that was simultaneously material technology and structural organization. EXPLOR was designed to produce still and moving pictures for research, educational, and artistic purposes. Its name implies a generative operation that employed "randomness" to simulate various processes in two dimensions: "other potential uses of EXPLOR are the generation of highly detailed patterns for experiments on vision, and simulation of some of the 'visual phosphenes,' such as squirming checkerboards or fringe patterns, which a person sees when he closes his eyes and presses upon them."[26] It was a system engineered to produce a variety of variable motifs. Two-dimensional patterns were designed and input into the computer, which produced sequential outputs whereby "each of the images generated is a two-dimensional array of white and black dots."[27]

The program could switch among several modes. It could test output to a paper printer and do a normal output run to the microfilm printer. It could understand the surface as a "wrap" (a torus "with opposite edges connected") or as a kind of window (a view onto a larger plane "in which case an extra 4 units of margin are computed, preserved and updated but never output").[28] It also was able to switch modes of unit arrangement from square to hexagonal. But most important, it allowed for an element of randomness that was entirely unlike the randomness of BEFLIX. Within BEFLIX, randomness was contained entirely within the frame so that characters could be randomly selected for display on a given surface. In EXPLOR, randomness emerged during sequential operations—from frame to frame. EXPLOR thus functioned generatively in a way that BEF-LIX had not. A command called "twinkle" that Knowlton added exempli-fies this aspect. As Knowlton described it, the computer stores positional information for each dot, and the programmer "specifies which of these characters are to be output as black and which as white dots, and which are to 'twinkle,' i.e., be chosen at random (probability = 1/2) frame by frame, to be black or white."[29]

Knowlton gives a number of examples of EXPLOR and the permutations it is capable of generating. The first example is crystallization: "etching, annealing, and nucleation" begin with either one-half or one-third white points scattered on a black background.[30] The program "agitates" one-sixth of the white spots above, below, right, or left of the black ones by turning them black and simultaneously turns white one-sixth of the black spots next to the white ones. The program then "coalesces" by turning the black spots within mainly white areas white and by doing the reverse for the white spots in predominantly white areas. The process is iterative, with the coalesce operation performed twice after each agitation.[31] Another example is "computation and output of the hexagonal mode, used here for simulation of snowflake crystallization. Each snowflake starts from a nucleus of a B totally surrounded by A's; growth is either regular or probabilistic, and into spots adjacent to either one or two crystallized spots, the latter choice being determined at random each time through the loop."[32] Another option was the "cyclic transliteration of randomly positioned sets of squares within squares, where sets overlap, more complicated and subtle patterns emerge."[33] In each of these, simple elements perform scripted behaviors, but what emerges is unpredictable. Lines twist, curve, and meander. Con-cise instructions give rise to complicated pictures and patterns.

Pixillated Pleasures

As Knowlton was writing the set of macros that made up EXPLOR, Lillian Schwartz was working to push the limits of this language with her first computer-animated film, *Pixillation* (1970). Because EXPLOR was not entirely finished, Schwartz felt that she could not make the entire film using computer animation alone. Thus, in addition to learning computer processing, she taught herself film animation, processing, and coloration, all new realms for her. *Pixillation* emerges as a fascinating example of "making do" that brings together hand- and computer-animated sequences into a captivating rondo of call and response that evokes the possibilities and limitations of each in turn by means of their juxtaposition. The four minutes of *Pixillation* mark a particular historical moment with an uneasy fusion of the mechanical and the organic. With this film, Knowlton programmed the microfilm plotter to emulate something that it was not and frankly could not be—a blocky, bitmapped screen. Schwartz fused this imagery with hand-colored animations and recorded images of crystal growth—both made through generative processes suggested by Knowlton's EXPLOR language. These processes, in turn, fed back into the writing of the language itself, as Knowlton described programming the computer to emulate natural processes such as crystallization.

Pixillation is an acknowledgment of a certain impossibility. It invokes the limitations of BEFLIX and suggests a thread of computer animation that would move far past the capabilities of the microfilm plotter. But it nevertheless emerges as a uniquely generative artwork. The title of the film invokes the pixel—the dot on the computer screen, the small indivisible square that formed the basis of the digital image after the advent of bitmapping. The title, *Pixillation*, here seems to denote the computational process that Schwartz learned using BEFLIX, the process to which the image of Deborah Hay had been subjected. Schwartz described this process as a "technological pointillism." By dividing an object into pixels or enlarging it so that the viewer can discern the individual pixels making up the image, the undergirding structure of the digital images is exposed in a way that frustrates any straightforward presentation of visual coherence. PXL is additionally the name of the command that Knowlton used in EXPLOR to set up "specific pair transliteration"—the "twinkle" effect that shimmers throughout Schwartz's film. Finally, the noun *pixillation* has mid-nineteenth-century cultural origins as a state of whimsy, bemusement, or mental unbalance. A common example of this use was the phrase "pixillated pleasures." It is a hallucinatory state, a state of unregulated pleasures, a bewilderment and bothering of the mind and the eye. The term's past and present lives are both apropos for the films Schwartz made at Bell Labs, and particularly in the sequence of works she produced with the S-C 4020.

Pixillation has three registers of imagery. The first orients the others and is the computer-generated animation created with EXPLOR and the microfilm plotter. Schwartz drew patterns on graph paper and then used

EXPLOR to code pixel-like blocks that became generative shapes once input into the computer. The process, as mentioned, was relatively blind. She had to wait until the full processing was done and the image sequences were output to 35 mm film before she could see precisely what she would get. The original shapes she designed were transformed, frame by frame, through the operations of EXPLOR. The sequences that emerged demonstrate the generative possibilities that are possible through procedure and constraint leavened with a certain amount of randomness and unpredictability.[34]

Second, in addition to the S-C 4020 output, Schwartz created a number of animation sequences in the traditional frame-by-frame method using a 16 mm film camera mounted on an animation stand. These brief sequences were extensions and counterpoints to the computer animation. They came about as the result of a series of improvisations: oil colors and plastic paints were poured and spread on glass, manipulated with brushes, fingers, palette knives, and compressed air. Dry colors were added to the oils, and further layers of colored glass were added and illuminated with projected light to create a variety of optical effects. When she found an image she liked, she used stop-action photography—exposing a frame and then repainting parts of the image before exposing another frame, and so on. Although the specificity of film animation was new to her, the compositional process was not wholly dissimilar from the process she had employed in creating her kinetic sculptures with their colored pulses of transparent fluids.

Third, in addition to these processes of generative animation, Schwartz arranged for the lab, under the direction of Charles Miller, to produce microphotography of crystal formations for use in the film. In this process, crystalline material enclosed in a small glass cell was moved across a temperature gradient while a microscope-mounted motion picture camera recorded the patterns of growth.[35] Their colors were obtained by allowing these recordings to be "placed between crossed polaroids, a scientific method of coloration."[36] Her goal was to create shapes that resonated with the shapes she was creating in the computer frames with Knowlton. After the frames were generated, she used an optical bench to color-match the black and white computer images to the colors of the stop-motion images.[37]

Schwartz built up image sequences from these frames, first imaginatively and then using an optical printing process to reduce the 35 mm output of the S-C 4020 to 16 mm. Schwartz worked with Bruce Cornwell to layer and suture the motion sequences together according to a score she had written out by hand. The still images produced by the S-C 4020 were thereby turned into the flashing animated sequences that they were always intended to be. Schwartz and Cornwell then added color filters to the black and white sequences and additional color filters to the hand-animated sequences to pull them into closer alignment with the newly colorized black and white sequences. Finally, working with Cornwell to selectively color her animations, Schwartz was able to step-print "stroboscopic and ecstatically complex motion manipulations" to create her finalized films.[38]

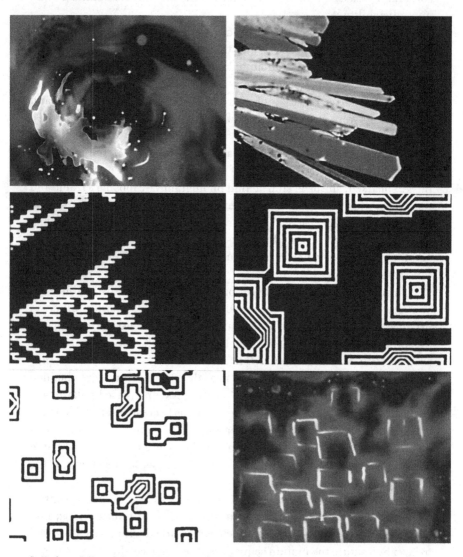

Stills from Lillian Schwartz, *Pixillation* (1970).

Pixillation opens with a title sequence whose block letters and repetitive squared patterns articulate their origin in the computer and microfilm plotter. The film begins in black and white—reflecting the native output of the S-C 4020—before switching to a red whose hypersaturation seems to announce its after-the-fact layering. Electronic sounds crackle over it, a bit like water drops but with a recognizably artificial edge. Several soundtracks eventually were produced for the film, but one written by Gershon Kingsley using an analog Moog synthesizer best maps onto the tension inherent in the film.[39] Kingsley's music gives an irregular pulse to the clustering. Like the imagery, it moves between the recognizably synthetic and the seemingly organic. After a few moments, the imagery abruptly shifts. Instead of recognizably computational squares, a wash of liquid color churns across the screen. Its patterning is dramatically different from the prior imagery: it is recognizably organic rather than machinic. A stream of liquid black splits the frame, and then glowing pink squares—clearly hand-traced rather than computer-generated—begin to appear in bursts. These skewed squares glow like warped neon. Suddenly, there is a strobing intercut of computer-generated squares. While the hand-drawn squares skewed slightly into angles, the computer generated squares are hyperbolically mobile, pulsing and moving across the frame.

As the film continues, the intercutting between artisanal and computational imagery speeds up. The soundtrack accelerates. As the images of the crystals appear, growing regularly and steadily, different types of imagery begin to run, overlap, and coalesce. Watching becomes an experience of flashes and afterimages. Patterns are consistently at the edge of legibility; they clarify and then obscure. Constantly shifting colors and registers in a play of difference, they are difficult to track or fix. The work continues to get louder, faster, and jitterier. At various points, the patterns shift and reverse color, producing a composite image on the retina that is not unlike the optical effects of pointillist painting that inspired Schwartz. Blue and white go to purple. As red disappears, its afterimage continues unabated. The film becomes a meditation on the creation and disintegration of visible forms that occur in a space somewhere between the eye and mind.

The film is a rush—aggressive and fast-paced, bordering on both violence and the sublime. Images echo one another. At times, the film seems to surpass the two-dimensional screen by provoking a hallucinatory experience of three-dimensional depth. But above all, it persistently returns our attention to the essential fracture between two very different types of images. It took Schwartz and Knowlton two months to create the eighty-five black and white frames on the computer. Simultaneously, she created more than fifteen hundred frames by hand animation.[40] The computer-generated sections display the effects that Knowlton made possible, which harness randomness to programmatically generate the unexpected.[41] Counterintuitively, the mechanical, computer-generated images of growing lines and squares and simulated crystals move smoothly and continuously, while the hand-made liquid animations do not. Schwartz intentionally undercuts the continuity of the latter by dropping frames so that the bubbling colors take on a staccato rhythm. The effect is strangely unnerving: a curious organicism accedes to the inorganic, while the organic is punctuated by a machinic jitter.

Like *Pixillation*, *UFO's* (1971) begins with shifting patterns weaving over each other in brilliant colors. It is a short film, only about three minutes long. Initially, the textures of the film, the woven patterns, are more obviously computational than *Pixillation*: the individual dots that Schwartz had been interested in manipulating when she arrived at Bell Labs are strongly visible. But then primary shapes—circles and half moons—begin to flare on the screen in red, yellow, green, and blue. The screen behind the circles blazes yellow, orange, black, and blue. The pace is relentlessly quick, and the circles, careening across each other, seem to move in a three-dimensional orbit—an effect enhanced by the stroboscopic flares that frame the images. As individual colors start to blur together, they create strange new perceptual effects: there is a startling purple, a fuchsia, a luminous midnight blue, each pulsing in turn. The soundtrack speeds up into an electronic wash. The patterns—psychedelic invocations of traditional carpet motifs, waving horizontal lines, and elaborate crystalline structures—come back into play as the shapes continue their scintillation. Then it is abruptly over, leaving only an emptiness filled with ghostly afterimages and a lingering affect.

Unlike *Pixillation*, *UFO's* does not rely on a juxtaposition of machinic and hand-done animation. Instead, the basic shapes generated by the computer are fused with color in post-processing. With *UFO's*, Schwartz started experimenting, haphazardly at first but then more concertedly, with calculated stroboscopic effects. She started editing in completely black frames between the color images. As she pointed out, the standard speed of twenty-four frames a second meant that individual frames passed too quickly for the spectator to see—and, indeed, the black frames she inserted were not precisely visible to the viewer.[42] Or rather, they were not noticed by the viewer as separate frames. Their appearance, their duration was too brief. But their existence intensified the colors they bounded, which henceforth seemed brighter, more saturated, more colorful. She called this "a major breakthrough in color saturation" achieved by "seducing the eyes to continue watching what they would otherwise avoid.... I never gave the brain enough time to consider not watching the film."[43] Schwartz was surprised by the reactions that viewers had when the film was shown at the Whitney Museum of American Art in New York. People reported experiencing headaches and hallucinations. It was described to her as "LSD without the drug."[44] A neurologist at the screening requested a copy of the film to induce seizures in his patients with epilepsy. He wanted to use it to train them to detect the aura that preceded a seizure with the hope of controlling it.[45] Schwartz even describes how "a pilot friend once told me that *UFO's* flicker rate was similar to the dangerous trance-like 'flicker vertigo' that can afflict helicopter pilots who stare at moving propeller blades."[46]

UFO's relies heavily on these "flicker" effects that are generated from the conjunction of different blocks of color on the film strip to produce a quasi-hallucinogenic experience. These effects experiences are not represented in the film but take place in the perceptual system of the spectator—as Paul Sharits put it, in "the electrical-chemical functioning of [the viewer's] own nervous system."[47] Looking to 1960, Peter Kubelka's *Arnulf Rainer* offers an origin point. It is comprised of pure black and clear celluloid, which are deployed in rapid-fire alternation. Its variously accelerating and decelerating "flicker" was immediately acclaimed (and denounced) for being able to bring about such powerful physiological and psychological effects in its spectators—including, but not limited to, migraine headaches, nausea, epileptic seizures, anxiety, exhilaration, and euphoria. This somatic element was highlighted, even parodied, by the notice displayed at the beginning of Tony Conrad's 1966 film *The Flicker*:

> WARNING. The producer, distributor and exhibitors waive all liability for physical or mental injury possibly caused by the motion picture 'The Flicker.' Since this film may induce epileptic seizures or produce mild symptoms of shock treatment in certain persons, you are cautioned to remain in the theater only at your own risk. A physician should be in attendance.[48]

This statement of somatic risk is couched as a legal disclaimer. It nominates the effects of the image sequences—its inducements and controlling aspects—in the tones of corporate, technocratic rationality, thus highlighting an overarching sense of danger that is sometimes attributed to the controlling elements of postwar technology.[49] Bob Lehman wrote of the physical sense of Schwartz's film, "It is strange to feel your body physically moving" despite sitting still. Amos Vogol wrote that it was "overpowering" and stated that

> what is even more ominous is that while design and action are programmed, the "result," in any particular sequence, is neither entirely predictable nor under complete human control, being created at a rate faster (and in concatenations more complex) than eye and mind can follow or initiate. Our sense of reality is thus disturbed not only by the filmmaker but also by the machines we have produced.[50]

Vogel's insight is that the essential disturbance of the film is created by an awareness of the machine processing that undergirds its creation. In a similar vein, the Whitney Museum of American Art's press release claimed that "the computer creates a nearly subliminal experience of abstract reality. The stroboscopic spheres in the second half of the film have been specifically created to affect the viewer's brain rhythm and induce a mild state of Alpha consciousness."[51] Both statements are conjoined in their understanding of these films as modeling a form of essentially technocratic control that is intimately related to its computational construction.

Programmed Visions

According to Schwartz, the restriction imposed by the microfilm plotter to black, white, and simulated gray levels—its "colorless nature"—pushed her obsession with color ever further. A year after *UFO's*, Schwartz screened *ENIGMA* (1972). With this film, Schwartz wanted to use simple black and white images to create the positive perception of color.[52] In creating these effects, she drew on the experiments that Edwin H. Land had performed at Polaroid, whose research can be traced to Johann von Goethe's theory of edge color, published in 1810.[53] *ENIGMA* is a choreography of rectangles, described by one viewer as "going into a museum and looking at thousands of Mondrians in every imaginable shade of color."[54] Rectangles are built up and broken down in stages, continually flaring and strobing on the screen. The initial portion of the film is entirely in grayscale, and the programming for the film simply controls the size, position, and brightness levels of the rectangles. Smaller and larger shapes are built, and the screen constantly strobes in between black and white. Shortly into the film, the effect that Schwartz sought becomes clear: the rapid shifts between black and white push the viewer into seeing color in between the articulated shapes. When the lines move and intersect enough, the viewer starts "to perceive saturated colors between the lines."[55] It is an uncanny effect: a concentrated set of afterimages lead the eye to see ghosted colors that are not quite there. The viewer is given even more cause to doubt the veracity of her vision when, a minute into the film, Schwartz starts to deploy color more directly. Emerging initially in ghostly fringing patterns, it gradually develops into full-frame hypersaturated colors and finally divides into discordant and flickering blocks of color. These intersect and interact in unpredictable ways because Schwartz's color is highly dependent on the saccadic motion of the eyes—jerky and uncontrollable—over the space of the screen.

Toward the end, the work moves into an odd, involuntary three-dimensionality, deploying some of the moving-square patterns that characterized *Pixillation*. These squares seem to hover over the surface of the rectangles. The effect is not unlike Julesz's stereoscopes, only now it takes place on a singular flat screen without the special-purpose glasses. Fittingly, the Bell Labs technical report on *ENIGMA* does not describe it as a film but situates it in the context of "experiments in combining various filters to produce the spectrum of color," suggesting that the sequences used to induce psychological and physical effects eventually could be part of a computer language and coded into the final programming."[56] In other words, they position it as an experiment in programming—computer programming, of course, but also, and perhaps more significantly, the programming of a human subject by the computer through the generation of particular physiological and psychological effects.

Schwartz's films set up a topos of circuits, feedback loops, pixels, and grids. They are in dialogue with the substantial transformations that are being wrought on vision and visuality by the shift from analog to digital in this era. As such, they mark the intrusion of the material conditions, visual forms, and cultural problematics that attended the rise of mass computerization in the 1970s, tracing a steady trajectory away from the photographic.[57] For Schwartz, *Pixilation* led her steadily away from the photographic image and toward a form of abstraction that she understands as fundamentally computational or informatic. It led her toward an interrogation of the S-C 4020 as a gridded screen of grays and, more significantly, toward its basis in black and white.

Her last film with the S-C 4020 pushes the furthest into its capabilities and produces something that is surprisingly modernist in its insistence on an aesthetic of reduction—of stripping down to what are understood to be the primary supports of the given medium. It takes some of the tricks of hand animation and uses them in the service of work that is thoroughly modernist in a way that prior work with the hybrid apparatus was not. In her earlier work, Schwartz used a vocabulary of simple shapes and hysterical colors to make films that explored the generative possibilities of the EXPLOR language and the specific capacity of microfilm linked to a CRT. Where film segments motion analytically, the S-C 4020 builds motion through the accretion of frames. By *Googolplex*, she moves past using hand coloration and instead uses the computer to create color flares in the eye of the viewer. The S-C 4020 continued to be used until the mid-1980s in a number of laboratories, but Schwartz's early films in some ways had already pushed the capabilities of the machine to their limits and, in so doing, generated something both fascinating and anomalous.

Like *ENIGMA*, *Googolplex* (1972) was inspired by Edwin H. Land's experiments at Polaroid in color perception. It was also inspired by her encounters with Béla Julesz, his experiments with "cyclopean perception," and his theory of vision as something that occurs in the brain rather than in the retinal processes. It is set to a field recording of African tribal music, all pulsing beats and chanting.[58] Where *ENIGMA* is structured with rectangles, *Googolplex* is composed and managed with strobe. *Googolplex* develops complex patterns from computer-generated lines, squares, and

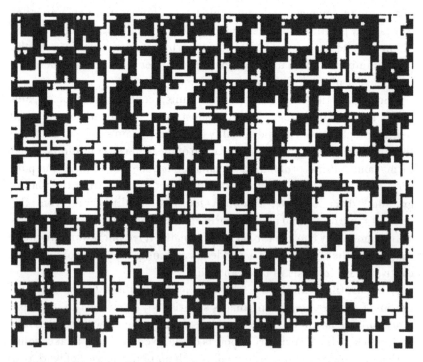

A still from Lillian Schwartz, *Googolplex* (1972).

circles. The patterns overlap into hieroglyphics. One reviewer described it as composing a new language—a computer language that is slowly taught as it is depicted.[59] Although Schwartz progressively inserted color into *ENIGMA*, *Googolplex* remained colorless—a condition that Schwartz evoked as a truth of the machine that she had to contend with. Nevertheless, even in its monochromatic construction, *Googolplex* still provokes hallucinatory outbursts of color—to bemuse the eye and perplex the brain.

The film is accomplished and playful. Thick straight lines combine with dozens of circles in flashing patterns. The strobe between black and white is continual. As the film proceeds, color fringing and then full color starts to appear to the viewer. Around and about the blocked lines and squares, there are bursts of static. Squares move minutely from frame to frame, faster than the eye can cleanly differentiate. As the squares stagger from side to side, rapidly alternating, the result is a motion in space that generates a hallucinatory depth.

ENIGMA and *Googolplex* are Schwartz's last films that focus on imagery made with the S-C 4020. Later films were photographed off of a computer monitor as Schwartz worked with a revolutionary interactive color processer—a joystick designed by Michael Noll and controlled with a program written by Knowlton. With these works, she finally left behind the specificity of the S-C 4020 and moved into interrogating a machine that had become steadily more complex and hybridized.

A Computer Aesthetic

Although Bell Labs consistently situated Schwartz's work as computer graphics and viewed it as part of a trajectory of experimentation with the computer as a specific apparatus, Schwartz initially situated her work in relation to experimental film. She was concerned with the progression of frames through a projector to create animation. Schwartz aligned her work with early pioneering artists in the field such as Viking Eggeling, Hans Richter, Walter Ruttman, and Oskar Fishinger, who had created experimental, abstract animations on film by all manner of invention, "from scratching patterns directly onto film to reshaping clay between shots."[60] Going even further, Schwartz was fascinated by the ways that Eggeling and Richter created "a visual symphony of abstract forms interacting with one another" and argued that her "EXPLOR was ... a modern restatement of the Eggeling-Richter philosophies."[61]

Yet Schwartz's work has been noted only infrequently by film scholars, who have tended to find it less formally innovative than its earlier precedents. William Moritz, for instance, has written that pioneers "like Stan

VanDerBeek and Lillian Schwartz ... both used Ken Knowlton's Beflix program to create numerous 'computer graphic films' which all look painfully alike, awkward in the accretion of oozing grids."[62] This was not entirely their fault, Moritz claimed, for "most artists have relied on software packages prepared by a technician or endemic to a particular hardware system. Their artistic compositions had to cope with the parameters, demands and limitations of a program over which they had no control."[63] Malcolm LeGrice disapprovingly describes Schwartz as an exponent of the so-called computer film who fails to remain true to the essential dictates of her chosen medium—using the computer "only to produce isolated sequences of abstract imagery which are then later combined and transformed according to aesthetic principles at variance with the intrinsic capacities of the computer."[64]

Moritz and LeGrice both point to something crucial about Schwartz's work. These works are not "films" per se so much as works of computational art that use film as an effective informational substrate. Schwartz is indeed stuck with the "parameters, demands and limitations of a program," but she also is stuck with the inherent parameters, demands, and limitations of the computational hardware—the S-C 4020 platform, consisting of a computer, Charactron screen, and microfilm printer. Schwartz develops what Douglas Davis later suggested was an "indigenous computer aesthetic" in contrast to what he derided as "fall out art, made by men whose commitments are elsewhere."[65]

Paradoxically, Schwartz's allegiance to her chosen medium, contra LeGrice, necessitated her particular form of "intermedia" creation. The materialist attention she brought to the S-C 4020 required her to attend to the complex, differential nature of its mechanical bricolage. In late modern aesthetic criticism, intermedia art was often condemned, in terms originally offered by Clement Greenberg, as "that particular form of widespread artistic dishonesty which consists in the attempt to escape from the problems of the medium of one art by taking refuge in the other."[66] Following Greenberg, midcentury modernism was typically understood as a process of reduction. But although works such as *Pixillation* are deliberately hybrid, problematizing the idea of the medium through a complex intertwining of forms, *ENIGMA* and *Googolplex* have harnessed this hybridity to work toward an almost straightforward interrogation of what computational form might be. They are probably as close to a strictly modernist conception of computer animation as you can get. Their idea of a computational aesthetic that is specific to the apparatus is one that develops at an uneasy intersection between the viewer and the generative process. Pulsing and straightforwardly manipulative, they blister the eye.

By the mid-1960s, the heyday of medium specificity had already passed. At a symposium in 1966, VanDerBeek talked about the idea that painting was dead, and everyone laughed and mocked him. But VanDer-Beek did not mean that the practice of applying paint to canvas would not continue—simply that the medium-specific conception of "Modernist Painting" programmatically articulated within Clement Greenberg's 1961 essay of that name no longer served as an unquestioned reference point for the contemporary generation of artists. If painting would continue (which, of course, it would), it would be by reinventing the idea of painting outside the framework of medium-specificity as a kind of "painting by other means."

Schwartz's work can thus be understood as resolutely untimely, for it remains quite profoundly invested in the specificity of the platform she is utilizing, even as it is no longer clear what the "specificity" of such a complex and hybrid "medium" as the S-C 4020 must necessarily entail. Yet her blind process pushed her steadily toward a hallucinatory black and white and toward what was arguably the most medium-specific work produced on the S-C 4020. After this film, she might be understood as having abandoned medium-specificity all together, employing a range of devices to create work characterized by an interactive use of color and animation. But that first film, *Pixillation*, was a recognition of impossibility for both Knowlton and Schwartz. An inquiry into what the microfilm recorder could *not* do, it juxtaposed precise squares with oil and water painting. *Googolplex*, in which she does not use color, is a meditation on the eye, the possibilities of imagination in viewing film, and the ways in which the computer can enable the seeing of that which isn't actually there. It investigated the critical blindness of working with a time-lapse apparatus by visual tricks that take place in the eye of the viewer. It is a gorgeous exploration of the possibilities inherent in constraint.

Conclusion

During the 1960s, the Stromberg-Carlson name dominated computer graphics. Prior to 1960, only a few hundred plotter printers were being used, and it is estimated that fewer than a hundred CRT screens were available for interactive display by 1964.[1] Despite these low numbers, by 1962 interest in the S-C 4020 had grown to the point that a dedicated user group called Users of Automatic Information Display Equipment (UAIDE) was established. This group was large enough to sponsor an annual conference where new techniques in computer graphics were presented and to publish and disseminate the conference proceedings. E. E. Zajac and Kenneth Knowlton's research, for example, was initially printed in the proceedings. The first conference took place in October 1962 and featured seventy-nine individuals from thirty-nine companies. By 1970, individual sessions were being attended by as many as 150 people.[2] But by 1974, the S-C 4020 had already fallen out of favor at Bell Labs and many other corporations, and UAIDE was folded into the National Microfilm Association.[3] No single machine upgraded or replaced the S-C 4020. Rather, various alternative technologies supplanted it, over the 1970s and after.

In 1963, after the first UAIDE meeting, General Dynamics produced a publicity film for the S-C 4020, promoting it as the herald for a future of graphical computing—a machine that "accepts digital information and reproduces it in forms familiar and usable." The film, called *The Mark of Man*, explains how the machine (which it calls a "computer recorder") works, detailing the intricate interrelationship between the Charactron tube, microfilm camera, and photo recording camera that "together with logic, power, and drive circuitry" form the S-C 4020. The film begins, as one does, with a cartoon of a bearded caveman wearing a loin cloth and using his fingers to paint on the wall. The voiceover tells us that

> From earliest times, man had made his mark. At first, his mark was on the walls of caves. With his own finger, he drew pictures of the animals he hunted. As man changed from hunter to farmer, his marks became stylized. Using chisel or brush, he developed symbols, alphabets, and languages. Man used marks to pass information from person to person or from generation to generation. Information recorded was retrieved for essential decisions. For example, the calendar became the guide for planting and harvesting crops. Through the ages, man recorded information to use again and again. The things he recorded, the law, history, mathematics were the things that brought pattern and order to his life. The history of civilization is the history of man's ability to record, to communicate, and to manipulate marks made to represent patterns and ideas.
>
> Always in making marks, there is a moving object. Today most marks are made by a type slug, a print hammer, a moving drum, or some mechanical device. Man now has electronic digital computers. These machines sort, transform, and generate information at unprecedented speeds. The speed of computers is so great that mechanical mark-making devices are inadequate. Their speed is limited by the inertia of mechanical parts. The parts moving at high speeds have impact loads, vibrations, and rapid wear, producing a need for constant maintenance. Mechanical printers make only the marks cast in their printing mechanism. They cannot position marks at random. The mechanical plotter requires setup and calibration time. Typically, it is slow and does not title or annotate its charts.
>
> Probably the best answer to this need to make marks faster and with more versatility is to use an electron. Electrons are the moving parts of digital computers. They account for the speed of these machines.
>
> Electrons are the moving parts in a new generation of machines that produce information. They make marks at speeds impossible for mechanical devices. They are capable of unlimited versatility in producing this information. For recording information from digital computers, General Dynamics electronics uses a device called the Charactron shaped-beam tube.... The Charactron can do any complex combination of lettering and drawing that man himself can do with

his own hand. But the Charactron tube by itself does not make permanent marks. Its image is volatile and disappears when the electron beam stops and the phosphorescence fades. A means is needed for recording this image permanently. The S-C 4020 computer recorder, designed and built by General Dynamics Electronics in San Diego, provides the means for permanent recording of Charactron tube images. It accepts digital information and reproduces it in forms familiar and usable to people. The S-C 4020 is at the forefront of the new generation of machines that write information.[4]

In twelve minutes, the film builds a trajectory from cave paintings to computer pictures. Animated figures detail progress: hieroglyphs are superseded by medieval manuscripts, then by typeset print, and eventually mechanical typewriters. But these machines are beset by friction and mechanical decay. They are insufficiently fast and insufficiently versatile. So the film offers a final stage appropriate to the digital computer: the volatile electrons the moving parts in a new generation of computers, can be used to make any complex combination of letters and pictures that man could make by hand.

The voiceover offers an ideal computation that is easy, fast, and frictionless. It suggests that maintenance will not be required and that an infinity of marks are possible—anything that can be imagined. The film reaches optimistically toward horizons without limit. Magnetic tape drives spin, computer switches light up, rockets take flight. This is the future as drawn by the S-C 4020. The previously invisible is suddenly, astonishingly, visible. The short film makes clear that computers of the future will be machines oriented toward the graphical and the visual. But it ties the graphical capability of the computer directly to the microfilm plotter, presenting it as the single best option for computer graphics.

This advertisement suggests such a different history for computer graphics that it is difficult to imagine it from a present that seems inevitable. This lineage does not track toward interactivity. It imagines computers with switches instead of screens. It imagines machines that are opaque to us in different ways from the ones that we use today. Looking at this advertisement, we can almost imagine a different history of computer graphics. But it is hard to step outside a trajectory that sees our current state-of-the-art computing as natural and inevitable. The S-C 4020 offers us another way of looking to the present by suggesting that we look at component parts rather than complete machines. It argues, implicitly, for the ways in which the "computer" and "computer graphics" meant fundamentally different things in 1963, 1971, and 2010. Its distance and opacity suggest that history is necessary to reconfigure the present. The peripheral orientation insists that cultural, historical, and machinic contexts are necessary. The S-C 4020 is not what we thought we knew about computer history. It is an instrumental machine with a noninstrumental history.

Looking at the work produced at Bell Labs with this machine throughout the 1960s, we find a complicated historical materiality tied in with this unique platform. This work emphasizes a dialogue between blindness and visibility. It is generative but not interactive in the ways that we have come to think about interactivity. This was work that shifted registers—moving from Bell Labs to art gallerys to the pages of popular newspapers and magazines. In each of these contexts, different elements were emphasized, but the marks of a singular process were visible for those who chose to look.

Notes

Introduction

1. Figures in 2014 dollars adjusted for inflation.
2. For a lively account of this history, see Jon Gertner, *The Idea Factory: Bell Labs and the Great Age of American Innovation* (New York: Penguin, 2012). See also Peter L. Bernstein, *Three Degrees above Zero: Bell Labs in the Information Age* (New York: Scribner, 1984).
3. The special-purpose software created for the S-C 4020 at Bell Labs became the basis of operations with the platform in a variety of locales.

Chapter 1: What Was a Microfilm Plotter?

1. General Dynamics advertisement, personal collection of author.
2. Paul N. Edwards, *The Closed World: Computers and the Politics of Discourse in Cold War America* (Cambridge, MA: MIT Press, 1997), 99–101. See also Thierry Bardini, *Bootstrapping: Douglas Engelbart, Coevolution, and the Origins of Personal Computing* (Palo Alto, CA: Stanford University Press, 2000), 86–87; Jan Hurst, Michael S. Mahoney, Norman H. Taylor, Douglas T. Ross, and Robert M. Fano, "Retrospectives I: The Early Years in Computer Graphics at MIT, Lincoln Lab, and Harvard," *ACM SIGGRAPH Computer Graphics* 23 (5) (1989): 19–38.
3. "Pushbutton Defense for Air War," *Life*, February 11, 1957, 62.
4. Jonathan Crary, *Techniques of the Observer* (Cambridge, MA: MIT Press, 1990), 147.
5. Alexander R. Galloway, *The Interface Effect* (Cambridge, MA: Polity Press, 2012), 13.
6. Edwards, *The Closed World*, 131. Also see Eve Meltzer, "The Dream of the Information World," *Oxford Art Journal* 29 (1) (2006): 115–135.
7. Edwards, *The Closed World*, 86.
8. Ibid.

9. Hurst et al., "Retrospectives I."
10. Ibid.
11. Ibid.
12. Ibid.
13. Edwards, *The Closed World*, 69.
14. S. H. Boyd and C. W. Johnson, "The Presentation of Alphanumeric Information," in *Illumination and Visibility of Radar and Sonar Displays: Proceedings of a Symposium Sponsored by the Armed Forces NRC Committee on Vision*, ed. Robert Heath Brown (Washington, DC: National Academy of Sciences, National Research Council, 1958).
15. Ibid.
16. Ibid.
17. IBM Military Products Division, "Introduction to AN/FSQ-7 Combat Direction Central and AN/FSQ-8 Combat Control Central" (Kingston, NY: IBM, 1959).
18. At this time, Joseph T. McNaney was at Consolidated Vultee Aircraft Corporation. General Dynamics Corporation acquired Vultee in 1953 and renamed it the Convair Division. General Dynamics merged with Stromberg-Carlson in 1955, shifting the Charactron project from Convair to Stromberg-Carlson's Data Projects Division. In 1969, the Data Projects Division split off and became a subsidiary of General Dynamics as Stromberg-Datagraphix, which continued to develop screens based on the initial Charactron screen as well as microfilm products intended as computer peripherals. See also Ben Ferber, "The Use of the Charactron with Era 1103," paper presented at the the the Eastern Joint Computer Conference: New Developments in Computers, 1956. See also Stromberg-Datagraphix training manual, personal collection of author.
19. Jackie Potts, "For the Computer Gourmet: Graphics" (Bethesda, MD: Naval Ship Research and Development Center, Department of the Navy, August 1974).
20. Eric Barbour, "The Strange World of Memory Tubes," *Tube Collector* 6 (5) (October 2004): 5–12.
21. Joseph T. McNaney, "The Charactron," *Proceedings of the IRE* 40 (2) (March 1952): 231.
22. P. Battey, R. Meijia, P. Baynes, E. Hairston, D. Hardy, and E. Cuthill, "S-C 4020 Microfilm Recorder Programming Manual I," Department of the Navy, David Taylor Model Basin, Applied Mathematics Laboratory, 1961, 2. See also Computer Sciences Corporation, "S-C 4020 Microfilm Recorder User's Manual" (1966); Potts, "For the Computer Gourmet: Graphics."
23. Stromberg-Datagraphix Training Manual, personal collection of author.
24. Paul Ceruzzi, *A History of Modern Computing*, 2nd ed. (Cambridge, MA: MIT Press, 2003), 74. Magnetic tape and punchcards continued to be used in tandem, however, with programs written on punchcards and translated to magnetic tape.
25. Bharat Bhushan, *Mechanics and Reliability of Flexible Magnetic Media* (New York: Springer, 1992), 20.
26. Paul Ceruzzi, *Computing: A Concise History* (Cambridge, MA: MIT Press, 2012), 39.
27. DatagraphiX Training Manual, 85, personal collection of author.
28. Ibid.
29. Frank Dietrich, "Visual Intelligence: The First Decade of Computer Art (1965–1975)," *Leonardo* 19 (2) (1986): 163.

30. John J. Kalagher, "Micromation: Its Impact on the Photocomposing Industry," *Electronic Composition in Printing: Proceedings of a Symposium*, ed. Richard W. Lee and Roy W. Worral (Washington, DC: Center for Computer Sciences and Technology, National Bureau of Standards, 1967), 37–38.

31. Stromberg-Carlson advertisement, "Only one computer output device gives you all three ...," personal collection of author.

32. Meijia et al., "S-C 4020 Microfilm Recorder Programming Manual I."

33. H. Garbanati, "Micro-Photography," *The Photographic News for Amateur Photographers* 1 (6) (1859): 262.

34. H. Garbanati, "Negatives of Valuable Documents." *American Journal of Photography* 1, (7) (1858): 100–102.

35. John Douglas Hayhurst, *The Pigeon Post into Paris 1870–1871* (self-published by the author, 1970).

36. Ibid.

37. Ibid.

38. Gene Youngblood, *Expanded Cinema* (New York: Dutton, 1970), 196.

39. *First* is a fraught designation. Other films claim this title, but it was the first film at Bell Laboratories to demonstrate the capability of the S-C 4020 for making computer graphics films.

40. E. E. Zajac and J. A. Lewis, "A Two-Gyro, Gravity-Gradient Satellite Attitude Control System," *Bell System Technical Journal* 43 (6) (1964): 2705–2765.

41. James R. Hansen, *Spaceflight Revolution: NASA Langley Research Center from Sputnik to Apollo* (Washington, DC: National Aeronautics and Space Administration, 1995), 188.

42. After the launch of *Telstar 2*, Bell Labs exited the satellite-development business.

43. E. E. Zajac, "Film Animation by Computer," *New Scientist* 29(1966): 348.

44. Ibid.

45. Ibid.

46. Ibid.

47. We might compare this with the heavy, complex robotic apparatus that Michael Snow employed for his 1971 film *La Region Centrale* to ensure that no camera movement was repeated in the 180-minute work.

48. Youngblood, *Expanded Cinema*, 222.

49. Ibid., 196.

50. Jasia Reichardt, *Cybernetic Serendipity: The Computer and the Arts* (New York: Praeger, 1969), 67.

51. C. G. Watkins, "When Two Worlds Collide," http://www.sidianersatzvanes.com/supplemental/when-two-worlds-collide-2.

52. Zajac, "Film Animation by Computer."

53. Keith Jack and Vladimir Tsatsulin, *Dictionary of Video and Television Technology* (Amsterdam: Newnes Press, 2002), 186.

54. Ceruzzi, *Computing*, 47.

55. Ceruzzi, *A History of Modern Computing*, 73.

56. IBM, "Mainframes Product Profiles: 7090 Data Processing System," http://www-03.ibm.com/ibm/history/exhibits/mainframe/mainframe_PP7090.html.

57. IBM, "7090 Data Processing System Technical Fact Sheet," October 4, 1960, http://www-03.ibm.com/ibm/history/exhibits/mainframe/mainframe_PP7090.html.

58. Ceruzzi, *A History of Modern Computing*, 74.
59. Ibid.
60. Zajac, "Film Animation by Computer," 346.
61. Ibid.
62. Ibid., 347.
63. This modality of filmmaking bears a resemblance to structural film, which incorporates ideas of film as system and the creation of families of films based on particular general principles.
64. Zajac, "Film Animation by Computer," 347.
65. Ibid., 349.
66. J. W. Sinden, "Synthetic Cinematography," *Perspective* 7 (1965): 287–288.
67. Ibid., 280.
68. Ibid.
69. Ibid.
70. Ibid.
71. Ibid., 282.
72. Roland Barthes, "The Photographic Message," in *Image-Music-Text*, trans. and ed. Stephen Heath (New York: Hill and Wang, 1977), 17.
73. See also Hyungmin Pai, *The Portfolio and the Diagram: Architecture, Discourse and Modernity in America* (Cambridge, MA: MIT Press, 2002), which contains an interesting discussion of photography and the diagram in relation to architectural practice.
74. Wolfgang Lefevre, *Picturing Machines 1400–1700* (Cambridge, MA: MIT Press, 2004).
75. Gilles Châtelet, *Figuring Space: Philosophy, Mathematics and Physics* (Dordrecht: Kluwer, 2000), 11.
76. Ibid.
77. Ibid.
78. Anthony Vidler, "Diagrams of Diagrams: Architectural Abstraction and Modern Representation," *Representations* 72 (2000): 9.
79. Barthes, "The Photographic Message," 17.
80. This moves toward Harun Farocki's recent work on computer vision, as well as the recent analyses of Lev Manovich and Alexander Galloway.

Chapter 2: Art Ex Machina

1. Michael Rush, "No Longer an Orphan, Video Art Gives Itself a Party," *New York Times*, February 10, 2002, 35.
2. Leo Castelli, oral history interview, October 24, 1991, by Sharon Zane, Museum of Modern Art Oral History Program.
3. Exhibition announcement for *Computer-Generated Pictures*, April 6–24, 1965, Howard Wise Gallery, New York.
4. Unknown to Noll and Julesz, an exhibition of computer art (including pieces by Frieder Nake and George Nees) called *Computergrafik* had been held only a few months earlier in West Germany at the Technische Hohschule in Stuttgart. See A. Michael Noll, "The Beginnings of Computer Art in the United States: A Memoir," *Leonardo* 27 (1) (1994): 41.
5. Stuart Preston, "Art Ex Machina," *New York Times*, April 18, 1965, X23.

6. Ibid.
7. Ibid.
8. Ibid.
9. See "Computer-Generated Pictures," *New York Herald Tribune*, April 10, 1965, 8, and "Computer-Generated Pictures," *Time*, April 23, 1965, 6.
10. Noll, "The Beginnings of Computer Art in the United States," 41.
11. Ibid.
12. Ibid., 39.
13. Ibid.
14. A. Michael Noll, "Patterns by 7090," technical memorandum, Bell Telephone Laboratories, August 28, 1962, 1.
15. A. Michael Noll, "Computers and the Visual Arts," *Design Quarterly* 66–67 (1967): 65–71.
16. Ibid.
17. See Nick Montfort, Patsy Baudoin, John Bell, Ian Bogost, Jeremy Douglass, Mark C. Marino, Michael Mateas, Casey Reas, Mark Sample, and Noah Vawter, *10 PRINT CHR$(205.5+Rnd(1)); : GOTO 10* (Cambridge, MA: MIT Press, 2013), 117–146.
18. There were exceptions, and many took advantage of a certain amount of programmed randomness—Stan VanDerBeek's and Lillian Schwartz's work at Bell Labs in animated film, John Cage's large-scale performance *HPSCHD*, Alison Knowles's 1967 Fortran programmed poem "House of Dust," and Jackson MacLowe's LACMA-sponsored poetry experiments. Knowles's and Maclowe's works, in particular, utilized the chance operations generally associated with Cage but adapted them to the particular randomization that was possible with the computer.
19. Branden W. Joseph, "HPSCHD: Ghost or Monster?," in *Mainframe Experimentalism: Early Computing and the Foundations of the Digital Arts*, ed. Hannah B. Higgins and Douglas Kahn (Berkeley: University of California Press, 2012), 149. See also Branden W. Joseph, *Random Order: On Robert Rauschenberg, Artist, and the Neo-Avant-Garde* (Cambridge, MA: MIT Press, 2003).
20. Allan Kaprow, "One Chapter from 'the Principles of Modern Art,'" *It Is* 4 (1958): 52, cited in Branden W. Joseph, "Chance, Indeterminacy, Multiplicity," in Julia Robinson, Yve-Alain Bois, Liz Kotz, and Branden W. Joseph, *The Anarchy of Silence: John Cage and Experimental Art* (Barcelona: Museu Dart Contemporani de Barcelona, 2010).
21. Erwin Panofsky, *Tomb Sculpture* (New York: Harry Abrams, 1964), 26–27.
22. A. Michael Noll, "Human or Machine: A Subjective Comparison of Piet Mondrian's 'Composition with Lines' (1917) and a Computer-Generated Picture," *Psychological Record* 16 (1) (1966): 1.
23. Ibid.
24. Ibid.
25. Noll, "The Beginnings of Computer Art in the United States," 39.
26. The year 1965 also saw the publication of an article by Max Bense, translated as "Generative Aesthetic Projects," which addressed some concerns that were similar to those raised in Noll's work. It was not available in English until 1968. See Max Bense, "Projeckte Generativer Ästhetik," in *Rot 19, Computergrafik* (Stuttgart: n.p., 1965).

27. See the 1955 exhibition *Le Mouvement* at Gallerie Denise Rene in Paris.
28. Jon Borgzinner, "Op Art: Pictures That Attack the Eye," *Time*, October 23, 1964, 78–86.
29. William Seitz, *The Responsive Eye* (New York: Museum of Modern Art, 1965), 6.
30. William Seitz, "The New Perceptual Art," *Vogue*, Feburary 15, 1965, 141–142.
31. Ibid., 141–142.
32. Borgzinner, "Op Art."
33. Seitz, "The New Perceptual Art."
34. Not only had this problem gone unsolved, but something as supposedly straight-forward as the "persistence of vision" that undergirds the phenomenology of the film and televisual image (and thus much of visual culture of the twentieth and twenty-first centuries) is actually still only dimly understood from within the twenty-first century cognitive perceptual psychology.
35. Jonathan Crary, "Techniques of the Observer," *October* 45 (1988): 25.
36. Julesz references Wheatstone in a number of his works, including his landmark treatise Béla Julesz, *Foundations of Cyclopean Perception* (Chicago: University of Chicago Press, 1971; Cambridge, MA: MIT Press, 2006).
37. Oliver Wendell Holmes, "Sun-Painting and Sun Sculpture," *Atlantic Monthly* 8 (1861).
38. Wheatstone successfully rebutted Brewster's argument with the support of Elliot, who proclaimed that he had not invented the stereoscope. Brewster then looked further back to Jacopo Chimenti, an artist who had created two slightly divergent sketches of a young man with a plumb line and a compass. When Alexander Brown saw them side by side in 1859, he was able to blur his vision sufficiently to see them as a single image with stereoscopic depth. When Brewster was told this, he suggested that the drawings were made to be seen with a stereoscope created by Giovanni Battista della Porta, who had done work on the camera obscura. The debate between Brewster and Wheatstone is detailed in part in H. Ono and N. Wade, "Resolving Discrepant Results of the Wheatstone Experiment," *Psychological Research* 47 (3) (1985): 135–142. The debate is also documented in Nicholas J. Wade, ed., *Wheatstone and Brewster: On Vision* (London: Academic Press, 1983). On the Chimenti argument, see Nicholas J. Wade, "The Chimenti Controversy," *Perception* 32 (2) (2003): 185–200. After measuring the images, it became clear that they were not fully stereoscopic but merely pseudo stereoscopic.
39. Hermann von Helmholtz, *Science and Culture: Popular and Philosophical Essays* (Chicago: University of Chicago Press, 1985), 192.
40. David Brewster, "Optics," in *Edinburgh Encyclopaedia* (Edinburgh: Blackwood, 1821), 750.
41. Béla Julesz, "Stereoscopic Vision," *Vision Research* 26 (1986): 1602.
42. James J. Gibson, *The Perception of the Visual World* (Cambridge, MA: Riverside Press, 1950), 6.
43. Stewart Kranz, *Science and Technology in the Arts: A Tour through the Realm of Science/Art* (New York: Van Nostrand Reinhold, 1974), 91.
44. Ibid. Something of the temporality involved can be seen with John Cage's production of the *William's Mix* in 1952. This pattern-derived musical recording was made by individually cutting and splicing together tens of thousands of audiotape

fragments by hand, a process that took the composer more than three months of manual labor.

45. Béla Julesz and Joan E. Miller, "Automatic Steroscopic Presentation of Functions of Two Variables," *Bell System Technical Journal* 41 (1962): 670.
46. Julesz, "Stereoscopic Vision," 1602.
47. Julesz, *Foundations of Cyclopean Perception*, 3.
48. Ibid., xvi.
49. Ibid., 3.
50. Ibid.
51. Ibid., 6.
52. Ibid.
53. Ibid., 56.
54. A. Michael Noll, "Stereographic Projections by Digital Computer," *Computers and Automation* 14 (5) (1965): 32–34.
55. Ibid.
56. John R. Pierce, "Portrait of the Machine as a Young Artist," *Playboy*, June 1965, 150.
57. Noll, "Stereographic Projections by Digital Computer."
58. Ibid.
59. Ibid.
60. Ibid.
61. Ibid.
62. Pierce, "Portrait of the Machine as a Young Artist," 150.

Chapter 3: *Studies in Perception*

1. Ken Knowlton, "Portrait of the Artist as a Young Scientist," *YLEM Journal* 25 (2) (2005): 10.
2. Among other places, this story is recounted in Knowlton's "A Portrait of the Artist as a Young Scientist," ibid. *Nude*, the first of the *Studies in Perception*, is often reproduced but rarely seriously discussed. Johanna Drucker is among a number of others who dismiss it as "shockingly dull." See Johanna Drucker, "Interactive, Algorithmic, Networked: Aesthetics of New Media Art," in *At a Distance: Precursors to Art and Activism on the Internet*, ed. Annmarie Chandler and Norie Neumark (Cambridge, MA: MIT Press, 2005).
3. Henry R. Lieberman, "Art and Science Proclaim Alliance in Avant-Garde Loft," *New York Times*, October 11, 1967, 49.
4. Ibid.
5. *Some More Beginnings: An Exhibition of Submitted Works Involving Technical Materials and Processes Organized by Staff and Members of Experiments in Art and Technology in Collaboration with the Brooklyn Museum and the Museum of Modern Art*, Experiments in Art and Technology, Brooklyn Museum, Brooklyn, New York, 1968.
6. Leon D. Harmon and Kenneth C. Knowlton, "Picture Processing by Computer," *Science* 164 (3875) (1969): 19–29.
7. J. Hurst, M. S. Mahoney, J. T. Gilmore, L. G. Roberts, and R. Forrest, "Retrospectives II: The Early Years in Computer Graphics at MIT, Lincoln Lab, and Harvard," in *SIGGRAPH '89 ACM Panel Proceedings*, 39–73 (New York: ACM, 1989).

8. Knowlton and Harmon, quoted in Jasia Reichardt, *The Computer in Art* (London: Studio Vista Limited, 1970), 10.
9. Knowlton and Harmon, quoted in ibid.
10. Paul Ceruzzi, *A History of Modern Computing*, 2nd ed. (Cambridge, MA: MIT Press, 2003), 91.
11. K. C. Knowlton, "A Computer Technique for Producing Animated Movies," in *AFIPS '64 Proceedings of the Spring Joint Computer Conference*, 67–87 (New York: ACM, 1964).
12. Ibid.
13. Computer Sciences Corporation, "S-C 4020 Microfilm Recorder User's Manual," 1966, I-2.
14. Ibid.
15. K. C. Knowlton, "A Computer Technique for Producing Animated Movies," in *AFIPS '64 Proceedings of the Spring Joint Computer Conference*, 67–87 (New York: ACM, 1964), 85.
16. Again, note that the Charactron was a hybrid screen but intended primarily for the display of text.
17. Email conversation with Kenneth Knowton.
18. A circuit diagram is a graphical representation of an electronic circuit. It does not represent the physical arrangement of the wires but shows the connections being made. In other words, it patterns the flow of signals and power using a particular symbolic language. It is the starting point for fabricating, for example, printed circuit boards. After the connections are diagrammed, a physical arrangement of material that will allow these connections is generated.
19. David Mindell, *Between Human and Machine: Feedback, Control, and Computing before Cybernetics* (Baltimore, MD: Johns Hopkins University Press, 2002), 134.
20. Ibid., 135.
21. Claude Elwood Shannon and Warren Weaver, *The Mathematical Theory of Communication* (Urbana: University of Illinois Press, 1949), 18.
22. N. Katherine Hayles, *How We Became Posthuman: Virtual Bodies in Cybernetics, Literature, and Informatics* (Chicago: University of Chicago Press, 1999), 54.
23. Note on exhibition record sleeve, Tate Archive.
24. The show was intended to travel to the Corcoran Gallery in Washington, D.C., and the Exploratorium in San Francisco, but the version that did travel was disowned by Reichardt because a substantive portion of the exhibition was destroyed in shipping. See Jack Burnham, "Art and Technology: The Panacea That Failed," in *The Myths of Information: Technology and Postindustrial Culture*, ed. Kathleen Woodward (Madison, WI: Coda Press, 1980).
25. Jasia Reichardt, *The Computer in Art* (London: Studio Vista Limited, 1970), 22.
26. K. G. Pontus Hultén, *The Machine as Seen at the End of the Mechanical Age* (New York: Museum of Modern Art, 1968), 3.
27. Ibid.
28. It was also not material in the sense that material is linked to visibility. Of course, it was material—so that the materiality of the medium and medium-specificity that emerged from it could give way to a dematerialized conceptualism of a post-medium condition.
29. For a detailed analysis of this problematic, see Wendy Hui Kyong Chun, "On Software, or the Persistence of Visual Knowledge," *Grey Room* 1 (18) (2004): 26–51.

30. Hollis Frampton, "For a Metahistory of Film: Commmonplace Notes and Hypotheses," *Artforum* 10 (1) (1971); 32–35, reprinted in Bruce Jenkins, ed., *On the Camera Arts and Consecutive Matters: The Writings of Hollis Frampton* (Cambridge, MA: MIT Press, 2009), 136.
31. Arthur Drexler and Greta Daniel, *Introduction to Twentieth-Century Design from the Collection of the Museum of Modern Art, New York* (New York: Museum of Modern Art, 1959), 94, cited in Felicity D. Scott, *Architecture or Techno-Utopia: Politics after Modernism* (Cambridge, MA: MIT Press, 2007), 80.
32. Ibid.
33. Ibid., 81.
34. Harmon and Knowlton, "Picture Processing by Computer," 22.
35. Richard F. Lyon, "A Brief History of 'Pixel,'" Digital Photography II, IS&T/SPIE Symposium on Electronic Imaging, Paper EI 6069, 2006.
36. Alvy Ray Smith, "A Pixel Is Not a Little Square, A Pixel Is Not a Little Square, A Pixel Is Not a Little Square (and a Voxel Is Not a Little Cube)." Technical Memo 6, Microsoft Corporation, 1995.

Chapter 4: *Poemfields*

1. James Tenney, transcript of "The House of Dust Symposium," University of California, Davis, April 9, 2002, cited in Douglas Kahn, "James Tenney at Bell Labs," in *Mainframe Experimentalism: Early Computing and the Foundations of the Digital Arts*, ed. Hannah B. Higgins and Douglas Kahn (Berkeley: University of California Press, 2012), 135.
2. Robert Russett and Cecile Starr, eds., *Experimental Animation: An Illustrated Anthology* (New York: Van Nostrand Reinhold, 1976), 200.
3. Ken Knowlton, "Reflecting on Collaboration," *animation: an interdisciplinary journal* 5 (2) (2010): 200. Despite the obvious corollary to E.A.T.'s activities, VanDerBeek and Knowlton had met, instead, through a mutual friend.
4. Stan VanDerBeek, "New Talent: The Computer," *Art in America* 58 (1970): 86.
5. Ibid., 91.
6. Michael Noll, "The Beginnings of Computer Art in the United States: A Memoir," *Leonardo* 27 (1) (1994): 39–44.
7. Gene Youngblood, *Expanded Cinema* (New York: Dutton, 1970).
8. VanDerBeek, "New Talent: The Computer," 71.
9. Béla Julesz, *Foundations of Cyclopean Perception* (Chicago: University of Chicago Press, 1971).
10. Youngblood, *Expanded Cinema*, 247.
11. Stan VanDerBeek, quoted in Jasia Reichardt, *The Computer in Art* (London: Studio Vista Limited, 1970), 79.
12. Youngblood, *Expanded Cinema*, 247.
13. Ibid.
14. Ibid., 246.
15. Matthew Fuller, "Visceral Facades: Taking Matta-Clark's Crowbar to Software," http://bak.spc.org/iod/Visceral.html.
16. This brief sequence reminds us of the flicker effects that are present in the computer-generated moving pictures of the Whitney brothers. Flicker effects were the ground for works by Steina and Woody Vasulka and Paul Sharits, as well.

17. Liz Kotz, *Words to Be Looked At: Language in 1960s Art* (Cambridge, MA: MIT Press, 2007).

18. Eve Meltzer, "The Dream of the Information World," *Oxford Art Journal* 29 (1) (2006): 124.

19. Oskar Morgenstern, *The Great Number*, Austriannale, Palazzo dell'Arte al Parco, Milano, 1968, Museum of Modern Art Archives, NY, Information Exhibition Records, 2.56, cited in Meltzer, "The Dream of the Information World," 125.

20. Kotz, *Words to Be Looked At*, 138.

21. Marjorie Perloff, "'Concrete Prose' in the Nineties: Haroldo De Campos's 'Galxias' and After," *Contemporary Literature* 42 (2) (2001): 270–293.

22. Eugen Gomringer, "Concrete Poetry (1965)," in Mary Ellen Solt, *Concrete Poetry: A World View* (Bloomington: Indiana University Press, 1969).

23. Earlier in his career, Bense had hoped to realize a process for rationally generating images. He divided picture surfaces into a grid of tiny squares to investigate the connections between these individual elements and to devise an algorithm for future images. He never created a satisfactory process and turned to informational analysis. His system was appropriated by George Nees and Frieder Nake as a programming technique for art production.

24. Eugen Gomringer, *Zur Sache Der Konkreten* (St. Gallen: Erker, 1988).

25. Ibid.

26. Ibid.

27. Ibid.

28. Rosmarie Waldrop, "A Basis of Concrete Poetry," *Bucknell Review* 22 (1976): 141–151.

29. In some ways, *Poemfields* is a return to his first film *MANKINDa* (1957), which is essentially a long poem and a series of artistic processes that dissolve and recombine words. It was a mode of practice he did not use again until *Poemfields*.

30. VanDerBeek's innumerable unpublished poems bear a similar fascination with the animation of words and the malleability of signification.

31. Reichardt, *The Computer in Art*, 79.

32. Marshall McLuhan, *Understanding Media: The Extensions of Man* (Cambridge, MA: MIT Press, 1994).

33. Ibid.

34. Ibid., 45.

35. Ibid., 79.

36. Stan VanDerBeek, "The Cinema Delimina: Films from the Underground," *Film Quarterly* 14 (4) (1961): 5–15.

37. See Pamela M. Lee, *Chronophobia: On Time in the Art of the 1960s* (Cambridge, MA: MIT Press, 2004), 185. See also Gloria Sutton, "Stan Vanderbeek's *Poemfields*: The Interstice of Cinema and Computing," in *Mainfram Experimentalism: Early Computing and the Foundations of the Digital Arts*, ed. Hannah B. Higgins and Douglas Kahn (Berkeley: University of California Press, 2012).

38. Stan VanDerBeek, quoted in Reichardt, *The Computer in Art*, 79.

39. Stan VanDerBeek, quoted in ibid., 80.

40. Stan VanDerBeek, quoted in ibid., 79.

41. VanDerBeek, "New Talent: The Computer," 91.

42. K. C. Knowlton, "A Computer Technique for Producing Animated Movies," in *AFIPS '64 Proceedings of the Spring Joint Computer Conference* 67–87 (New York: ACM, 1964).

43. Ibid.

44. Stan VanDerBeek, "Culture Intercom: A Proposal and Manifesto," *Film Culture* 40 (1966): 18.

45. Ibid., 16.

46. Tono Yoshaiaki, *Stan Vanderbeek, Wizard of Expanded Cinema* (Tokyo: Kodansha, 1969).

47. VanDerBeek, "New Talent: The Computer," 91.

Chapter 5: Pixillation

1. The majority of the rest were shown in a second show at the Brooklyn Museum called *Some More Beginnings*. The nine selected pieces were shown in both locations. See "Love, Hate and the Machine," *Time*, December 6, 1968, 86–89.

2. K. G. Pontus Hultén, *The Machine as Seen at the End of the Mechanical Age* (New York: Museum of Modern Art, 1968).

3. See ftp://cm.bell-labs.com/who/cocteau.old/lillian/old/index.ep.html.

4. Lillian F. Schwartz with Laurens R. Schwartz, *The Computer Artist's Handbook: Concepts, Techniques and Applications* (New York: Norton, 1992), 6.

5. These works bear some striking similarities to the contemporaneous practice of the "postminimal" sculpture of Eva Hesse.

6. See Schwartz, *The Computer Artist's Handbook*, 7, 238.

7. Ibid., 12.

8. Ibid.

9. Ibid.

10. Ibid.

11. In 1969, AT&T executives commissioned Schwartz to make a promotional film for Bell Labs that would "improve AT&T's image on college campuses." See Walter Forsberg, "Lillian Schwartz Sees in Four-Dimensions," *Incite: Journal of Experimental Media* 3 (2011).

12. See Schwartz, *The Computer Artist's Handbook*. See also Carolyn L. Kane, "Digital Art and Experimental Color Systems at Bell Laboratories, 1965–1984: Restoring Interdisciplinary Innovations to Media History," *Leonardo* 43 (1) (2010): 53–58.

13. Interview with Lillian Schwartz by Walter Forsberg, printed in the booklet accompanying the *Orphans in Space* DVD, available at http://archive.org/stream/OrphansInSpaceBooklet_sm/Orphans_in_Space_booklet_low-res_djvu.txt.

14. B. Coffey, "In the Mind of ... Lillian Schwartz," *Computer Pictures* (January/February 1984): 52–56.

15. Schwartz, *The Computer Artist's Handbook*, 183.

16. This statement could readily be disputed, but it spoke to the role that she played in the Labs. See ftp://cm.bell-labs.com/who/cocteau.old/lillian/old/index.ep.html.

17. Schwartz, *The Computer Artist's Handbook*, 5. She is citing Meyer Schapiro on Seurat.

18. Ibid., 32.
19. Ibid.
20. Ibid.
21. Ibid.
22. Ibid., 34.
23. Ibid., 151.
24. It later was used for a variety of applications, including Béla Julesz's continuing experiments in vision, as well as teaching and research projects.
25. The program was designed for the IBM 7094 and the S-C 4020, but the initial implementation was a series of emulations—an IBM 360/50 emulating an IBM 7094 (with hardware-based convert instructions) and a Stromberg-Datagraphix 4060 using a hardware-based 4020 emulator. Both Schwartz and Harmon considered that they had worked on editions of the earlier machines and refer to them interchangeably. The majority of the material aspects of the microfilm plotter were identical. The primary difference was in the number of commands it could accept, but Knowlton and Schwartz limited themselves to those available with the original machine by working with the emulation.
26. Ken Knowlton, "EXPLOR: A Generator of Images from Explicit Patterns, Local Operations and Randomness," *UAIDE: Users of Automatic Information Display Equipment—Proceedings of the Ninth Annual Meeting* (San Diego, CA: Stromberg-Datagraphix, 1970), 560.
27. Ibid., 544.
28. Ibid., 545.
29. Ibid., 544.
30. Ibid., 559.
31. Ibid., 560.
32. Ibid., 562.
33. Ibid.
34. This was the unpredictability that the new wave of artists employing video recording technology in the late 1960s and early 1970s had begun to avoid. Rather than the traditional photochemical process of development with still and motion picture photography, whereby precise results remained unknown until often days later, video technology allowed for the continuous monitoring of the shoot in real time—radically transforming the possibilities and affordances of the moving image for contemporary art.
35. Lillian F. Schwartz, "The Artist and Computer Animation," in *Computer Animation*, ed. John Halas (London: Focal Press, 1974), 160.
36. Ibid.
37. Schwartz, *The Computer Artist's Handbook*, 153.
38. Forsberg, "Lillian Schwartz Sees in Four-Dimensions."
39. Dick Moore wrote a second soundtrack using a program completed at roughly the same time as EXPLOR. It was called GROOVE (Generated-Realtime-Operations-On-Voltage-Electronics) and used a computer, an analog synthesizer, and a speaker.
40. Schwartz, *The Computer Artist's Handbook*, 153.
41. Knowlton, "EXPLOR," 562.
42. Schwartz, *The Computer Artist's Handbook*, 115.

43. Ibid.

44. Ibid.

45. Interview with Lillian Schwartz by Walter Forsberg.

46. Ibid.

47. Paul Sharits, "Notes on Films, 1966–1968," *Film Culture* 47 (1969): 14.

48. See the beginning of Tony Conrad's *The Flicker* (1966).

49. See Felicity D. Scott, *Architecture or Techno-Utopia: Politics after Modernism* (Cambridge, MA: MIT Press, 2007).

50. Amos Vogel, *Film as Subversive Art* (New York: Random House, 1973), 118.

51. Press release, Whitney Museum of American Art, New York, February 17–23, 1972.

52. Schwartz was drawing on theories of perception developed by Edwin H. Land at Polaroid.

53. Schwartz, *The Computer Artist's Handbook*, 116.

54. Robert Lehman, "Mind Bogglers: 'Moceptions,'" *Today's Filmmaker* 2 (2) (1972): 6.

55. Schwartz, *The Computer Artist's Handbook*, 116.

56. Lillian F. Schwartz, "Motion Picture / Computer System for Visuals and Sound," Lillian Feldman Schwartz Collection, Ohio State University Libraries, 1970. See Kane, "Digital Art and Experimental Color Systems at Bell Laboratories."

57. Matthew Kirschenbaum, in "Vector Futures: New Paradigms for Imag(in)ing the Humanities," *Poetess Archive Journal* 2 (1) (2010), links bitmapping directly to photorealism in an extended contrast with vector graphics. Ron Burnett, in *How Images Think* (Cambridge, MA: MIT Press, 2005), links digital imaging most clearly to television. Lev Manovich, in *The Language of New Media* (Cambridge, MA: MIT Press, 2002), ties digital imaging and the figure of the computer to the cinematic image. William Mitchell, in *The Reconfigured Eye: Visual Truth in the Post-Photographic Era* (Cambridge, MA: MIT Press, 1994), interrogates the digital image in relation to the photographic. Vivian Sobchack, "The Scene of the Screen: Envisioning Cinematic and Electronic 'Presence,'" in *Materialities of Communication*, ed. Hans Ulrich Gumbrecht and K. Ludwig Pfeiffer (Stanford: Stanford University Press, 1994) ties it to electronic imaging, by which she means the televisual.

58. She experimented with three different recordings, as with *Pixilation*, to see how the different soundtracks would shift the viewer's experience.

59. Lehman, "Mind Bogglers."

60. Schwartz, *The Computer Artist's Handbook*, 151.

61. Ibid., 152.

62. William Moritz, "Visuelle Musik: Larry Cuba's Experimentalfilm (Visual Music: Larry Cuba's Experimental Film)," *Mediagramm, ZKM (Center for Art and Media)* 24 (1996): 12–13.

63. Ibid.

64. Malcolm LeGrice, *Abstract Film and Beyond* (Cambridge, MA: MIT Press, 1977), 80.

65. Douglas Davis, "The Artist and the Computer," *Newsweek*, September 13, 1973, 81.

66. Quoted in Kerry Brougher, *Visual Music: Synaesthesia in Art and Music since 1900* (London: Thames & Hudson, 2005), 82.

Conclusion

1. F.R.A. Hopgood, "Pioneering Images," paper presented at a meeting of the BCS Displays Group, San Diego, CA, December 1991.
2. Bob Hopgood, "Report on U.S.A. Visit, 1971," http://www.chilton-computing .org.uk/acl/literature/reports/p021.htm.
3. Ted Nelson, *Computer Lib/ Dream Machines*, self-published, 1974, 104.
4. Transcription from *The Mark of Man*. General Dynamics.

Index

Note: Page numbers in *italics* refer to illustrations.

Printed in the United States
by Baker & Taylor Publisher Services